ANTIQUE BUTTONS
Their History and
How to Collect Them

FRONTISPIECE

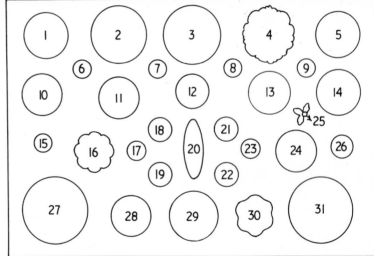

ANTIQUE BUTTONS

Their History and
How to Collect Them

PRIMROSE PEACOCK

Drake Publishers Inc. New York

LOC 73-1888796

ISBN 87749-235-2

Published in 1972 by
DRAKE PUBLISHERS INC
381 Park Avenue South
New York, N.Y. 10016

Printed in Great Britain

CONTENTS

1 and 2 Eighteenth-century buttons (by courtesy of the National Trust).
The buttons shown above and opposite come from the collection of the late Baroness
Edmond de Rothschild, now on display at a National Trust property, Waddesdon
Manor, Aylesbury, Buckinghamshire. The majority are in prime condition for their age,
and are among the small numbers of fine buttons on public display in Britain. Photo-
graphs by Peter Parkinson, FIIP, ARPS, London.
Among those shown are examples of jasperwear, cloisonné, enamelling, cut-steel work,
reverse painting, inlay work, jewel settings and 'habitat' buttons. All date from the late
eighteenth or very early nineteenth century, and although they may not be handled,

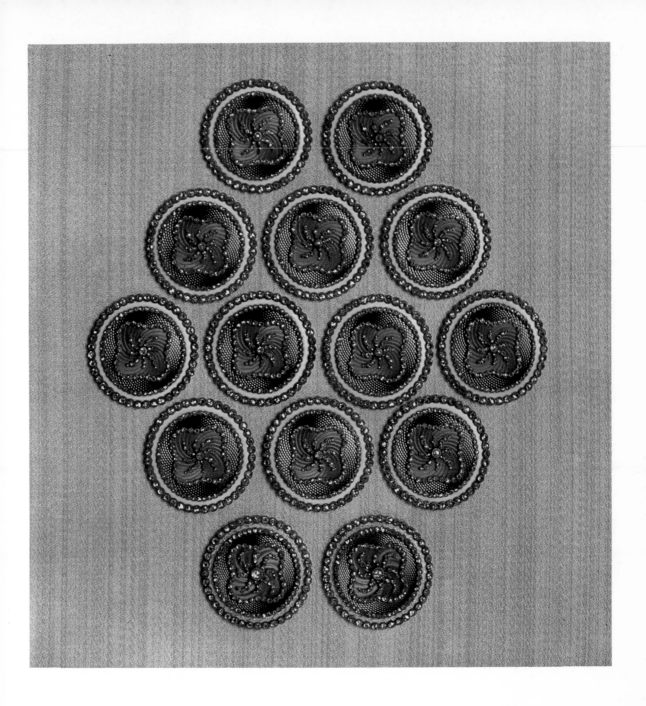

inspection with a strong lens suggested continental and oriental workmanship for all, including the jasperwear, which seemed darker and slightly coarser than Wedgwood items seen elsewhere. The 'habitat' buttons were made by placing small pieces of grass, seeds, etc under glass and it is not surprising that these have deteriorated with age. These buttons would have been made for use on men's coats, breeches and waist-coats, not for ladies' dress, and would have been individually designed to order, and produced largely by hand. Inspection of some of the cut steel shows a very high standard of handwork, and the painting is as good as that found on miniatures of the period.

INTRODUCTION

The object of this book is twofold: firstly, to introduce the hobby of button collecting to the British and to explain some of the ways in which the Americans have pursued it for the past thirty years; and secondly, to assist everyone by providing information on buttons made in Britain and Europe from 1800 to 1940. In other words, to further good Anglo-American relationships!

EXPLANATION TO BRITISH READERS

The hobby of button collecting commenced in America during the 1930s depression. Ladies were encouraged to hunt out old buttons, spend time arranging them artistically and learn about them. Mrs Gertrude Patterson, credited as being the first known collector, gave radio talks on her hobby. Since then it has grown rapidly, until now there are button collectors in every state, and many well-organized clubs.

Americans in general have an intense interest in collecting almost anything. The American home, far more than the British, is the centre of the social system, and much time is spent on it and its beautification. American women seem to have more leisure time and more money than their British counterparts, and generally enjoy entertaining at home. The majority make a conscious effort to maintain a youthful and attractive appearance throughout their lifetime and most succeed in remaining young in spirit until they die. It is not uncommon for smartly turned out 'girls' in their eighties to drive long distances to club events.

There are two main movements among American button collectors. The National Button Society of America has its headquarters near New York and is responsible for a bi-monthly *Bulletin*, button shows, conventions, and the encouragement of projects. An annual convention is held, and members enter for prize competitions, as do Women's Institute members in Britain.

The Just Buttons Museum at Southington, Connecticut, run by Mr and Mrs Victor Luscomb, is the headquarters of the *Just Buttons* monthly magazine. It is also a centre for teaching and hobby days. The Luscombs work on more flexible lines than the 'National' and encourage collectors to express their own personal taste. There are a number of state and city button clubs, which may be affiliated to one or both of the above organizations. Mrs Luscomb is also a button dealer and, like others in America, exhibits at shows, flea markets and sales.

The nearest British equivalent to button collecting is philately. Buttons are gathered and arranged in much the same way as we do stamps. Button collectors have built up their own language and terminology. A number of books have been written on the subject, the modern ones being well illustrated, but most writers are conscious of the difficulties of research on buttons that were made outside the United States.

EXPLANATION TO AMERICAN READERS

In Britain there are only a few isolated individuals collecting buttons. There are no collectors' magazines or clubs. Those few people who collect do so generally as the result of a visit to America, or an interest in costume. There is one established business in London selling old buttons, and a small number of antique dealers who sell to tourists or the dress trade. My own business has been confined to selling by mail order in America since 1968. British people buying old buttons are primarily interested in sets for use on clothing, as the custom of hand sewing and knitting is widespread.

The collecting of buttons has probably been overlooked in Britain due to the wealth of other types of *objets d'art* until recently available. However, British women are generally less attracted to clubs than Americans and have less time and money to devote to hobbies, with the exception of gardening! The British flower and vegetable garden demands much time, attention and love and is quite unlike the American yard—an area of unfenced lawn and shrubs.

British social activities are mainly centred outside private homes, as only a small minority can afford lavish entertaining or servants. The public house, bingo hall, religious and political group activities, or adult education courses tend to take the place of social meetings in homes. For those who prefer to stay at home, there is always television—and British television offers a wider range of programme content than do the US networks.

Finally a note for American readers on prices quoted in this book. All dollar prices given were calculated at 1 January 1971. Britain changed to decimal currency in February 1971, and, instead of using pounds, shillings and pence, commenced a new method of calculation. The pound sterling remained constant, the equivalent of $2.40, but is now divided into 100 new pence. Each of the former 20 shillings that made up the pound is now 5 new pence (5p), equal to 12 cents. British prices given in this book are therefore in the new currency, with the exception of those in historical quotations.

Many of the buttons on plate 3 are also illustrated on plate 41 and are discussed under that heading. They are shown again here as they form one of the most colourful groups of buttons, and splendidly illustrate the attractive possibilities of a button collection. To the uninformed the term enamel seems immediately to conjure up the idea of a valuable button, and items which bear no relationship to true enamels are often proudly presented by their owners as genuine.

Confusion frequently arises between true enamelling and enamel paint. The two buttons on each end of the bottom line but one are examples of pressed metal buttons which have been painted to represent enamels. This has been done deliberately, and although the buttons are perhaps a little better made than the painted metal buttons described on page 86, they are not enamels.

Other materials sometimes confused with enamel are painted glass, milk glass with or without outline design (see page 62), and ceramics.

One method of distinguishing a true enamel button from an imitation is to look at the back. True enamels normally have flat backs, whereas others show indentations in reverse from the pressed pattern on the front.

Enamel buttons are sometimes finished with a matt effect, as seen in the second and fourth buttons in the second row down. They are also by no means obsolete : the two buttons in the top row with white grounds and the girl's head in the centre of the page are modern productions.

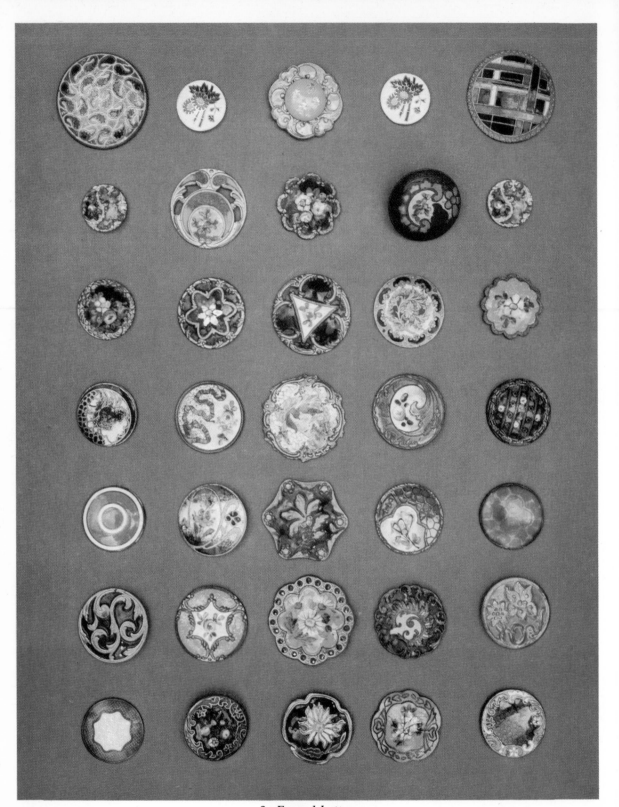

3 *Enamel buttons*

4 *A variety*

Key to plate 4

Anyone making a collection encounters a wide variety of items, some with greater merit than others, but all interesting in their own way. This page shows a typical selection including one or two slightly bizarre items.

1 *A modern example of a habitat button (see also page 7). Grain and lentils (now mouldy) have been encased under plastic with a wooden rim and metal loop shank. I would suggest the 1940s utility period as a date for this button—perhaps an ingenious idea during wartime scarcities?*

2 *Log button*

3 *Stamped celluloid with painted metal underneath*

4 *Thread button from Eire. The star of David design probably has no special significance*

5, 7 *Painted wooden buttons from the 1930s*

6 *Plastic patriotic button*

8 *Moulded-horn button showing a high standard of die-making*

9 *Vulcanite buttons with painted trim*

10 *Unusual button made from metal and glass. Black and mirror glass used over a white metal base*

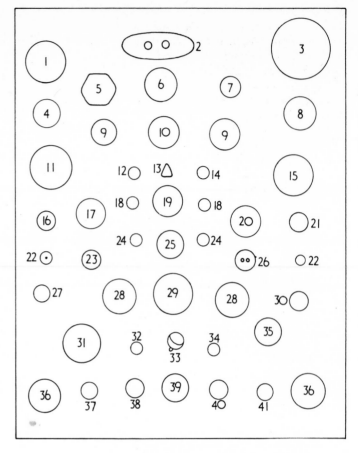

11 *Painted milk glass. See also page 62*

12 *Hollow blown-glass ball with self-loop shank. Very fragile and quite impractical. These buttons have been seen in a variety of colours, some with a pearl finish, and are also known in plastic*

13, 18 *Dorset thread high-top buttons. No 13 is an extreme example of the cone shape. (Also page 30)*

14 *Faceted glass ball*

15 *Pearl shell button with steel facets set in a brass rim. Mid-nineteenth century*

16 *Waistcoat button, printed on paper under glass*

17 *Milk glass. Marked 'Made in England' on the shank plate which is attached with adhesive. Such glass blanks were produced by glass-makers and then shanked or pinned by distributors according to taste, as buttons, brooches, etc. See also page 62*

19 *1953 coronation button by J. & J. Cash of Coventry. Woven rayon*

20 *Undyed horn with Royal Naval emblem*

21 *Semi-sulphide type of waistcoat button. From the 'road to ruin' series. See also page 60*

22 *Humble boot buttons*

23 *Undyed horn simulating plaited leather*

24 *Handpainted design on porcelain in metal mounts*

25 *Porcelain, with self-shank. Probably French c1900*

26 *Brass trouser button from one-time local tailor*

27 *Metal and celluloid*

28 *Eighteenth-century incised shell buttons with metal mounts and imitation jewels. Bought on a market stall, where unfortunately the owner, not realising their value, had allowed them to become damaged in a junk tray*

29 *Handpainted porcelain with self-shank. No indication of origin on the button which could be English or French. c 1860?*

30 *Inlay design on glass*

31 *Vegetable-ivory button with pearl centre. See also page 47*

32, 34 *Celluloid over wooden moulds*

33, 36, 39 *Agates*

35 *Abalone shell*

37 *Faceted carnelian*

38 *'Real bloodstone' in metal mount (Buttons Ltd)*

40 *Lapis lazuli*

41 *Carnelian in metal mount, marked gilt*

Key to plate 5
The small buttons forming the border are a selection from the many ball, charm-string and waistcoat buttons made from 1880-1930. See also pages 54-61. Paperweight buttons are shown at the centre top and bottom. The other buttons on this page are described below.

1, 22 Black glass, often mistakenly called jet. See page 49. No 22 has a matt finish and as it is marked 'depose' on the back it must be French. It is unusual for black glass buttons to be back-marked
2, 7, 9, 13, 15 Czechoslovakian glass buttons made in Jabonek during the 1930s. Taken from salesmen's sample cards of the period
3 Modern glass button with tennis motif
4, 19 Glass buttons with lustre trim. See also page 51
5 White milk-glass button with impressed and painted décor and four-way metal shank
6, 11 Unusual types of lacy glass buttons. See also page 51. No 6 has only a rim of backing paint and No 11 has had a tartan-type design applied with paint before the backing layer
8 Inlay design
10, 12, 14, 17 Metal buttons trimmed with glass brilliants. See also page 74. These four date from the 1890s and all have claw settings
16 Czech glass buttons with brilliant positioned by adhesive. 1930s
18 Pressed-glass head with gold-painted trim
20 Glass jewel glued to metal base. Fragile and impractical
21 Tiny spotted glass-ball button with two-way metal shank

13

5 *Buttons made of glass*

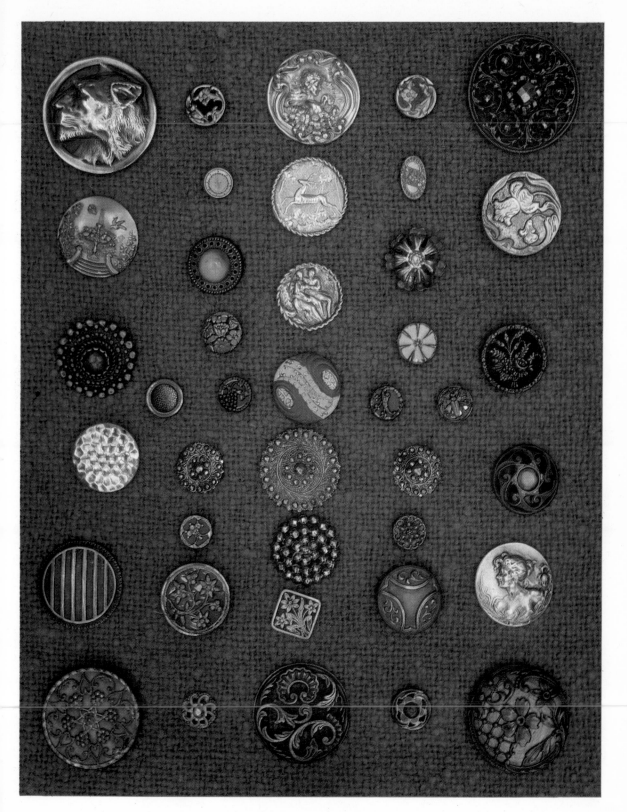

6 *Buttons made of metal*

Key to plate 6

All types of metals, ranging from gold to inferior alloys, have been used to make buttons. Those shown here represent a typical cross-section. Many of them are of types more fully described elsewhere in this book, where further examples are shown in black and white.

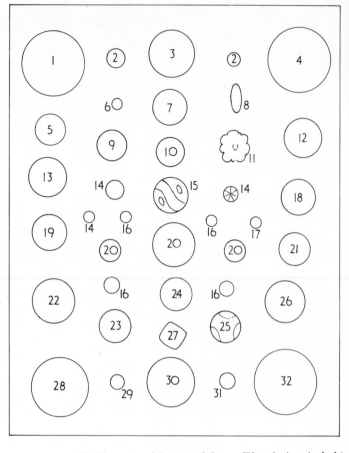

1 Stamped brass with loop shank
2, 18 Velvet backs
3 Hallmarked silver. Birmingham 1903. Maker L. & S. An unusual feature of this button, which was given to me by a dealer in Tipperary town, is the registration mark (405484) stamped on the front
4 Very well made bronze-finished button decorated with steel
5 Metal picture button in alloy. See also page 72
6 Silver and enamel button from a dress-shirt set. Marked sterling silver
7, 10 Unmarked stamped silver buttons, probably German. No 10 was a present from an Englishman who heard about No 3!
8, 16 Austrian tinies. See also page 78
9 Pressed alloy with glass 'jewel' centre. Probably Czech
11 Pressed metal button with gilt finish. Among many purchased from a retired draper
12 Two-piece metal with pressed design
13 Pewter-type alloy with glass jewel
14, 15, 21, 29, 31 Examples of painted metal buttons. See also page 86
17 Three-piece metal. Cut-out design with brass

finish over white metal base. The design is held in place with six small lugs
19 Beaten sterling silver over bone mould with self-shank. Birmingham 1905. Maker G. & C. Ltd
20 Matthew Boulton steel types from official court dress. Early 19th century. Some writers refer to all steel buttons as 'court buttons', but the term should only really apply to solid types
22 Heavy alloy button with stamped design
23 Escutcheon type marked 'Fast shank'
24 Matthew Boulton openwork steel type. See also page 25
25 Two-piece metal with pressed brass design
26 One-piece stamped brass design portraying a Gibson-girl type head. Charles Dana Gibson was a well-known illustrator at the beginning of this century who illustrated the adventures of a heroine of his creation—an early counterpart of the Daily Mirror's famous 'Jane'
27 Neillo work, black enamel used to fill the spaces in an etched design
28 White metal lacy pattern over celluloid
30 Heavy cut-out design on plated brass button
32 Cut-out pattern over painted metal

THE ARRANGEMENT
OF THIS BOOK

This book is primarily concerned with buttons produced in Britain during the period 1800-1940. Those made in European countries and widely imported are discussed in lesser detail, and American productions are mentioned so that readers there have a basis for comparison.

No attempt has been made to cover the productions or methods of every manufacturer during the period, or even to collect the finest possible examples. The buttons illustrated represent my personal collection made over a period of five years, together with a few donated or lent. They are the types of button which should be in the reach of any collector of average means. The companies discussed represent a typical cross-section; there are plenty of other buttons and other companies of equal merit.

The story of buttons during the period is the story of a group of people. Like all such stories it is influenced by the foibles of human nature. Every facet of social history is represented, and so it is no surprise to find that human greed, unpaid debts, broken hearts, oppression by dictators, all play their part, as do happy marriages, clever inventions, moral principles and hard work for its own sake. Perhaps the most striking characteristics of the button makers of the past were their tenacity and humour.

The period in question is divided into three sections. First the years 1800-1875 which from a manufacturing point of view can be likened to the gradual ascent of a mountain. During this time new methods and materials were discovered, and the industrial revolution resulted in gradual mechanisation. The majority of British buttons produced were primarily functional and utilitarian, when compared with eighteenth-century French output, but the pride of the workman in his job was reflected in the quality of the finished article.

The years 1876-1910 represent a plateau in manufacture and the zenith of the designer. Contemporary fashions called for numerous trimmings, including buttons, and the rapid automation of manufacturing processes resulted in a wide variety of decorative items using an equally wide range of materials and techniques.

After 1911, changes in fashion, World War I and the subsequent economic recession resulted in a decline in quality and variety. This period extending until 1940 is regarded as a descent period.

The fourth section deals with buttons of specialized collector interest, from various countries, and a few miscellaneous categories. Within each section buttons have been grouped according to the materials from which they are made.

Values

'Values' of buttons are quoted in some American books, and price guides to other works can be obtained. Americans, more than the British, like to know the value of what they possess, even if they have no intention of parting with it, regarding such knowledge as a type of insurance. They also make a careful study of patenting and the dates thereof.

17

Very few British people pay much attention to patents, but American publications list them carefully and owners record patent dates for items in their possession.

British readers are advised that values quoted in American books relate entirely to the American situation, which is different from that in Europe because (a) Americans have been seriously collecting buttons for thirty years, and have built up a certain amount of mystique around the subject; and (b) due to the relative youth of the country, old buttons are not as easily acquired in the US as they are in Britain. While I was in Texas during 1970 one collector drove 250 miles to see me, spent an hour choosing buttons and then drove home. She regarded the trip as a Sunday afternoon outing! In Britain driving twenty miles to the coast and home is considered a long way by many families.

Button collecting, like other hobbies, has its fads. If some particular type of button receives press publicity the price rises rapidly. If an unusual variety is included in a club project, inflation follows. Prices slump as rapidly. Good eighteenth-century buttons and fine examples of the nineteenth century will always be priced high, but others come and go. British readers are reminded that although the income of the average American is three or four times that in Britain, so is the cost of living. Petrol and tobacco are the only two major items that are cheaper in America.

People selling buttons in Britain (and they are few) tend to price according to appearance. I have been asked to pay £7.50 ($18) for six pretty enamel buttons, but at the same time 50p ($1.20) was considered adequate for six rare peacock-eye types. In America the same buttons would have been worth £10 ($24) for the enamels, but the others would have fetched approximately £4.15 ($10) each.

American price guides should be regarded as guides only, and used in much the same way as dealers use the catalogue issued by a leading firm of philatelists. The prices given are possibilities for mint specimens. Most buttons seen are worth less than one-quarter of the value.

A brief survey of fashion 1800-1940

In order to appreciate the design of buttons it is as well to have an idea of the type of clothing for which they were intended. Buttons were made primarily to complement the clothes to which they were attached and, while the methods and materials available governed initial output, it was the demands of fashion which were responsible for sales.

At the beginning of the nineteenth century women's dresses were of a pseudo-Grecian style reflecting French empire furniture and design. The wearing of buttons was then almost entirely a male prerogative, and these buttons were large gilt adornments.

During the 1830s the embryo crinoline made its appearance in the form of dresses with bell-shaped skirts and enormous sleeves. These were first worn with large brimmed hats, but after 1835 bonnets were favoured. By 1840 the large sleeve had been reduced, and an excessive fullness appeared in the skirt which grew progressively more tentlike until the climax was reached in 1865. At this stage women were finding great difficulty in entering and leaving transport!

By 1870 the skirt fullness had moved to the back and was supported by a bustle; the bonnet was replaced by a forward tilted hat. For men, gilt buttons were past history. The Florentine, or covered button, was worn almost exclusively on men's day clothes, waistcoats of the period often being trimmed with worked buttons of the Leek type.

In 1875 nipped-in waists appeared in women's fashions and, with them, many rows of small buttons from neck to hips. The fashion model of the day was constricted by a tight bodice with equally tight sleeves and a bulky skirt over a cage-like bustle. One male writer of the time commented caustically:

> Dressmakers load their work with ugly and senseless frills, which do not end anything, with bows which do not tie and buttons which are of no use. and are incapable of understanding the grace of simplicity. A dress is considered a perfect fit when a lady can neither raise her arms nor use her legs.

During the 1880s dresses gradually became more simple with reduction in skirt bulk, the jacket retaining the tight waist but extending to the hips. Contemporary pictures show numerous buttons. This is the period described as the plateau of decorative button making.

In 1890 the bustle had finally disappeared and the skirt had become narrow and close fitting at the hips. The emphasis shifted to the sleeve and for a few years the leg-of-mutton sleeve was in vogue. By 1900 skirts were more gracefully flared, hats were becoming enormous, and women were taking up sport. Outfits for bicycling, tennis and swimming were quite remarkable in their construction. Men started to wear knicker-bocker suits. The long period of national mourning for Prince Albert coupled with the tradition that widows should dress in black had resulted in a vast production of black buttons.

From 1900 to 1914 women's fashions were initially a continuation of the 1890s, but the Art Nouveau movement produced more relaxed draped styles, with numerous wraps, floating panels and other draperies. 1911 was the year of the hobble skirt, but this quickly disappeared as a result of the urge for feminine freedom and the growing suffragette movement. Males of the period were colourful Edwardian dandies, decked out in gay waistcoats and sporting accessories. Women peered from under cartwheel hats at the straw boater and check motoring cap.

World War I drove half the population into khaki uniform and the other half into mourning. Women began to take over work previously done by men, and clothing was adapted accordingly. Skirts became shorter and flared, but were still calf-length. Men not on active service favoured plus-fours and Norfolk jackets.

The 1920s saw women's knees exposed to the world for the first time, and with the Charleston came beaded dresses, flat chests, pyjama sunsuits and flowerpot hats pulled down over Eton crops. Easier transatlantic communication produced a vogue in Britain for anything American, including much considered risqué by the older generation.

In the 1930s styles were more modified, with skirts just below the knee, and more natural curves in place of the flat chest. Men strode about in Oxford bags, striped blazers and co-respondent shoes. The advent of World War II brought clothes rationing —and the termination of this survey.

ONE:
THE GRADUAL ASCENT
1800-1875

The Golden Age

> The oldest of the Birmingham buttons seems to have been a plain flat button, of the waistcoat size, which a hundred years ago (1750) were sold at 4/6 [54 cents] a gross, and which is still manufactured at 1/6 [18 cents] a gross. Then came a very large button, the size of half-a-crown, with ornamental devices on it; but this was dear. It was the gilt and plated button, introduced between 1797 and 1800, which made the great 'hit' in the trade. This became immediately fashionable, and continued so for a quarter of a century.

This is the opening paragraph of an article on the button trade in the *History and Description of the Great Exhibition 1851*. An example of the large button can be seen on the frontispiece (No 3). It is made from sheet copper, hand decorated, and has a loop shank soldered to the back. This type of button was worn throughout the eighteenth century, and is known to Americans as a Colonial.

The gilt and plated buttons referred to are known to collectors as Golden Age buttons, because of their colour and quality. These were made up from one or two pieces of metal. At the beginning of the nineteenth century the shanks were attached by a newly invented machine, but before that firms had been making up to 200 million button shanks by hand.

The secret of the button's beauty was in the gilding, and for this purpose it was customary to add five grains of gold per gross buttons to a mixture of mercury, brush it on the buttons, and then cook them in a furnace. After this they were burnished with bloodstone.

The Americans did not commence making such buttons until 1812, having then acquired a knowledge of the process by methods which would now be regarded as industrial spying! However they found that they could not produce buttons to the British quality even when they added additional gold to the mixture.

Golden Age buttons are usually stamped on the back—triple gilt, triple standard, double gilt, etc. This refers to the number of times they were dipped in the gilding mixture or the number of grams of gold used. In every trade there is a black sheep and in the year 1800 a trial took place in Birmingham, the centre of the button industry. A group of button makers had been carrying out a practice similar to a present-day infringement of the Trades Description Act: they had been making buttons of inferior quality and selling them as triple gilt. The trial caused much excitement and public interest. One of the spectators in the public gallery was a Mr Job Nott, who subsequently wrote a long letter to his cousin John, describing in detail the proceedings and result. Initially Mr Nott had some difficulty in gaining access, but after he had returned home for clean clothes he was admitted to the public gallery in company with a friend named Gubbins. The trial commenced at ten o'clock, and the accused were asked how they would plead. On the reply 'not guilty', the court proceeded to hear evidence from the prosecution. It appeared that a large quantity of buttons had been discovered hidden in a pit. These had been removed by a constable and taken to his house by horse and cart. After the constable, the next witnesses called were

> . . . some nice calculators from Soho (where you know they understand everything) who came to prove how much ought to be on every sized button, and when the Assay Master told them what was found on, they told them what was deficient to the thirty-third, one-hundred-and-twenty-eighth part of a grain, which seemed quite a surprising thing to me—but Gubbins told me their master who had taught them all to be clever, could tell to the twenty-five-thousandth part of a grain.

Evidence for the defence was submitted by a clerk who said he had given out all the gold needed, and by gilders who swore they had put it all on the buttons. A lengthy dispute followed between the Assay Master and other witnesses as to how many grains of gold were initially applied, and how many remained after processing the buttons.

The trial continued over two days, with various interruptions, and much discussion as to the precise meaning of the Metal Button Act of 1796 (regulating manufacture and sale of metal buttons). Finally, counsel for the prosecution made a lengthy speech in which he pointed out that the purpose of the Act was to protect the trade and not fetter it. He gave many examples of other places and countries where the passing of similar acts had ensured quality maintenance. He finished by saying: 'If masters were permitted to carry on such practices [marking buttons treble gilt when they were not even double gilt] and apprentice boys and journeymen witness it, can there be a greater inducement to swerve from the path of virtue?'

Apparently not, for when the verdict was given the following day the defendants were found guilty and fined £550 ($1,320) and costs. An appeal was made and unsuccessfully heard at Warwick, by which time costs had risen to £1,200 ($2,880). Mr Nott concluded his letter by saying that the button makers were considering a London appeal on a point of law, but that he thought they were wasting their time.

Bone and Ivory Buttons

The majority of bone buttons made during the nineteenth century were purely utilitarian and intended for underwear and household linen. They were made by cutting discs from the shinbone of animals and then punching or drilling holes in them and polishing. Such buttons were usually produced by companies which made horn buttons.

The four buttons shown at the bottom centre of plate 7 are turned bone, imitating ivory, and are late nineteenth century. They have metal loop shanks at the back. Bone can be distinguished from ivory by inspection with a magnifier: small black specks in the material indicate bone. The carving of ivory from elephant tusks was always a difficult job as the material fractured easily and was slow to work. An example of a carved ivory button, purchased in the USA and thought to be of oriental origin, is shown in the frontispiece (No 28). It has a self-shank.

The bone brace button was practically discontinued after the advent of vegetable ivory (page 47) and decorative bone buttons were never popular in Britain. In America most decorative bone buttons are either oriental imports or tourist items from Alaska.

The large engraved pearl buttons on plate 7 and the frontispiece (No 27) are known as coaching or sporting buttons and were worn during the eighteenth and early nineteenth century. These examples are inlaid with gold and mounted in pinchbeck. They could be of British or French origin. Pearl buttons are discussed in greater detail in a later section.

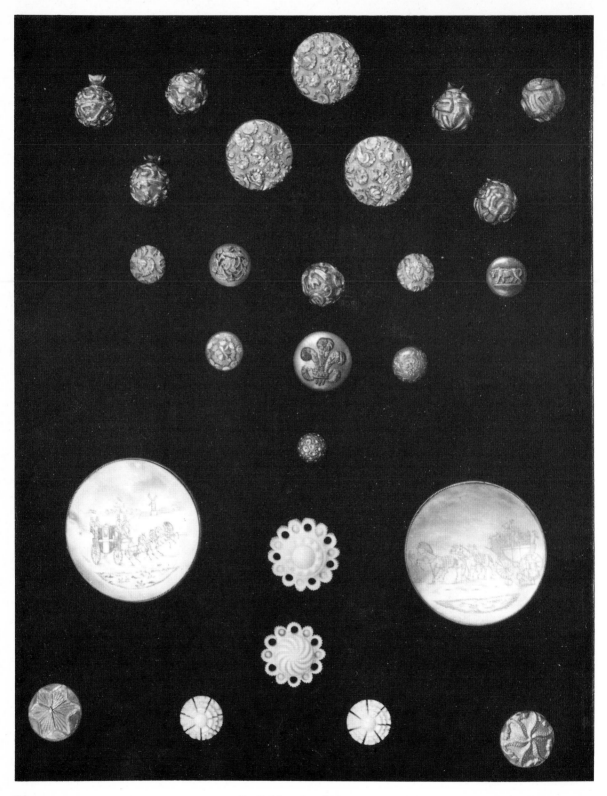

7 *Golden Age buttons*

The Chase

Man has long indulged in the 'sport' of hunting or chasing animals, and so it is no surprise to find that buttons depicting sporting events or bearing hunt club emblems were popular throughout the nineteenth century. The best of these were made during the period 1800-75, when it was usual for each button in a set to show a different design.

A large number of Birmingham button makers exhibited their wares at the Great Exhibition of 1851, and in the official catalogue these were described under class 22 with annotations by W. C. Aitkin. Sporting buttons were shown by Piggott & Co, St Paul's Square; Hammond Turner & Sons, Snow Hill; Allen & Moore, Great Hampton Row; William Elliott & Sons, Regent Street; and G. & William Twigg, Summer Hill.

Sporting buttons are fine examples of the engraver's art, showing incredible detail and lifelike portrayal. They are well worth collecting, either to mount for display or to wear, and look particularly attractive on knitted garments. An article of 1850 on button manufacture in Birmingham describes in detail the die-making process:

> What is this steel die, which is so much heard of, and so seldom seen? It is a block of metal, round or square, about four or five inches in height and rather smaller at the top than the bottom. It consists of a piece of soft steel in the centre surrounded by iron to prevent it cracking. The steel surface at the top is polished, and if it is intended for a medal is turned on a lathe. The artist sketches his subject upon it, from a drawing. When he is satisfied he begins to engrave. He rests his graver on another graver and cuts away very gently.

There follows a description of the engraving and hardening processes, and then the writer moves on to the room where mock-ups for the preparation of the original drawings are stored, and comments as follows:

> Think of the skill in animal drawing required for the whole series of sporting buttons, from the red deer to the snipe! Think of the varieties of horses and dogs, besides the game! For crest buttons, the lions and other animals are odd and untrue enough but, out of the range of heraldry, all must be perfect pictures.

The majority of sporting buttons are what the manufacturers of the day called shell buttons, but collectors now refer to them as two-piece metals. Another contemporary writer describes the joining of the two parts (this was also the method used for the two-piece Golden Age buttons):

> There are differences too, among convex buttons, some are of one thickness only, others are hollow, being formed from two blanks, one called the shell, the other the bottom, and named in consequence, shell buttons. The two parts of a shell button are brought together by the application of a die and punch. So completely do they act, that the edge of the shell is bent over and lapped down on the bottom uniting them thoroughly.

Collectors in America refer to pearl buttons as shell buttons—one example of possible confusion of terms, and a reason why collectors are advised never to purchase any button until and unless they have seen it, and are of one mind with the vendor.

The three chased buttons at the centre top of plate 7 are marked G. & W. Boggett, St Martins Lane, London; on each side of them are three unmarked spherical buttons; another of these is shown in the centre of the 3rd row. In row 3 the 1st left and 4th buttons are marked 'triple gilt' and the 2nd left 'Jennens London'. In row 4 the 1st left is marked 'gold lace', the centre one 'MS & JD'; the 3rd one and the small one below are unmarked. The two buttons at the bottom corners of the plate are marked 'triple gilt' and 'treble standard' respectively.

Background—velvet.

8 *Animal and sporting buttons*

Cut Steel

Buttons made of steel were worn on court costumes; they were bright and brilliant, the light gleaming from the many facets with which the button face was adorned, and immense prices were charged and paid. Matthew Boulton, who eventually aided James Watt, was in the early part of his career a manufacturer of steel buttons and buckles.

So wrote W. C. Aitkin in 1876 in a book entitled *British Manufacturing Industries*. James Watt was, of course, the inventor of the steam engine.

Some sources attribute the invention of the riveted steel button to Matthew Boulton of Birmingham, others maintain that such buttons were developed independently by British and French manufacturers, but there is no doubt that they became very popular during the eighteenth and early part of the nineteenth century as a substitute for the marcasite button made from pyrites. This in turn had resulted from manufacturers in eighteenth-century France seeking an imitation for diamonds.

The earliest steel buttons were made by riveting numerous polished steel facets to a prepared base plate. Then a Frenchman named Trichot produced steel buttons by stamping them from a single sheet and polishing the upper surface. This process, which was of course considerably cheaper and easier, was quickly adopted in Britain and after 1830 riveted buttons were less frequently seen. At the 1851 Exhibition steel buttons were shown by William Aston of Princep Street, Birmingham, and Smith, Kemp & Wright of Brierly Street West. Both these firms made numerous other types of buttons, but Astons are reported as using 5 tons of sheet steel annually for the production of light toys. (In the nineteenth century a wide variety of small metal objects such as buckles, clips, studs etc were called toys.)

At the time of the Exhibition there was apparently a shortlived attempt to revive the riveted steel button, and some were made with up to 300 facets or studs on the face. They were made by cutting a blank from sheet steel, curving it by use of a stamp and then perforating in a press. The studs and their pins were soldered and attached before the button was case-hardened and tempered in oil. The studs were then cut by wheels lubricated with emery and oil, before being polished with a variety of materials, the finest being putty. Steel facets were also used throughout the nineteenth century as trimmings, and steel pin-head shanks and rims were also popular.

After 1880 lustre glass (qv) replaced steel, and the majority of late Victorian and Edwardian shiny buttons are made from this material. Steel buttons are easily distinguished from glass: firstly they respond to a magnet, and secondly they are prone to rust. The rusting was the main reason why they fell into disfavour in the damp British climate. Once rusted they are almost impossible to clean, and even with the use of modern preparations can never be fully restored to their original state. The mere fingering of such a button is enough to start rusting.

On plate 8, in the top left and right corners are bronze-finished buttons marked 'H.J.M. Paris'. The small gilt fox head is marked 'extra superb'. The seven animal buttons encircling the centre and the steeple-chaser at the bottom are marked 'treble strand extra rich'. The large button in the centre is marked 'Engetragen' (twentieth century). The bronze-finish hare bears the name 'Firmins'.

At top centre and in the two bottom corners are unmarked hollow white-metal buttons of a type worn by American hunters.

Background—cross-stitch on linen crash.

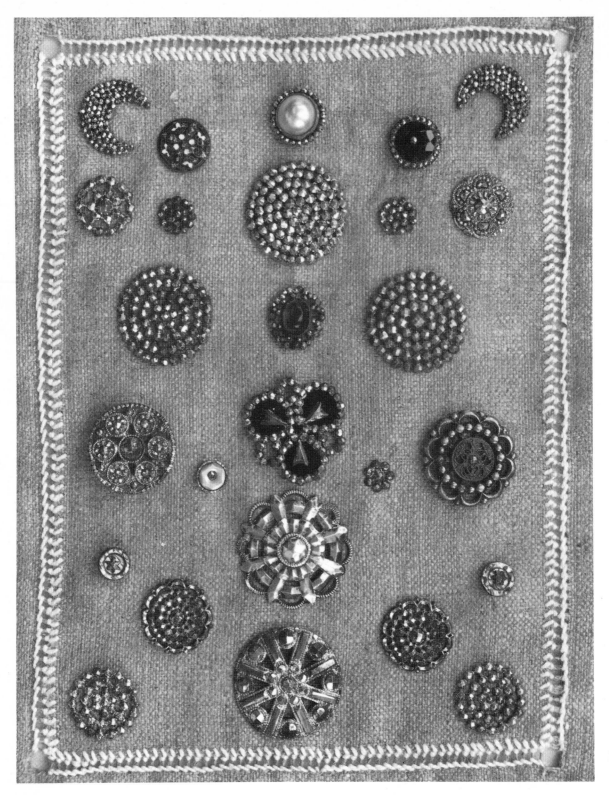

9 *Riveted and pressed steel buttons*

Inspection of the button back will usually indicate the method of manufacture. Riveted steel buttons have numerous small dots on the reverse side—these are of course the rivets. Pressed steel shows the reverse patterning. Glass buttons are usually flat and solid.

Towards the end of the nineteenth century many buttons were made from metal alloys in the manner of pressed steel. These do not respond to a magnet, and are less likely to rust. R. B. Rathbone writing in *The Art Journal* of 1909, speaks of old English steel buttons, and illustrates his article with examples from old sample cards of Messrs Jennens & Co. He indicates that these were originally made for eighteenth-century court dress. Steel buttons on such a dress, and also on early nineteenth-century costume, can be seen at the Museum of Costume in Bath, Somerset.

Fabric Buttons

The button made from thread and fabric was initially the main competitor to the metal button, and the cause of considerable tension in the trade during the first part of the nineteenth century. Fabric buttons in general have only small collector-interest due to their utilitarian nature, but they played a large part in the social history of the button makers.

Three types of fabric button were made during the period 1800-75: the Florentine or covered button, invented in 1802; the thread button, made in Dorset and Leek (Staffordshire), and handstitched over moulds or wires. Although quickly replaced by Florentine buttons for outer wear, the manufacture of types of thread button suitable for underwear and household linen continued until the 1850s before declining; and the linen button—this was parallel in development with the Florentine—continued well into the twentieth century.

There are also a few miscellaneous categories of buttons incorporating fabric, and these are considered here for convenience.

THE FLORENTINE BUTTON

Prior to 1800 the fashions of the day called for a bright array of gilt buttons on men's coats (though few, if any, buttons on women's wear). Then in 1802 came Mr B. Sanders and his first covered buttons: Sanders came to Britain from Denmark, having lost a fortune when Nelson bombarded Copenhagen in 1801. He initially set up a button business in Birmingham, but soon moved to Bromsgrove when he found the Birmingham people over-inquisitive. His first covered buttons had iron shanks, but the customers disliked them as they rusted, so he substituted shanks of catgut. However he was unable to patent this method, and found he was quickly copied. The flexible linen shank was invented by Sanders junior, who patented the process in 1825. The Florentine button was born, and so named from the silk with which it was initially covered.

The buttons shown on plate 9 represent both the riveted and the pressed methods of manufacture, the crescents at the top corners being good examples of the former, and the large button in the centre bottom of the latter. This plate also illustrates the use of steel shanks and rivets in conjunction with enamel work (2nd left), mother-of-pearl (top centre) and black glass (4th right); the trefoil-shaped button is of a type known to collectors as a velvet back (qv). Other examples of steel rivets and trimmings will be found elsewhere in this book.

Background—hemstitching on linen.

The end of the Golden Age was in sight, and the makers of gilt buttons were, not surprisingly, upset. They went so far as to send a deputation to London to support their claim for a monopoly, and managed not only to lobby the Duke of Clarence, the Lord Mayor and Members of Parliament, but also to gain the attention of George IV, who supported them by encouraging the wearing of gilt buttons. Flushed with success they returned to Birmingham in triumph, but then spoiled their reputation by using a cheaper method of gilding, which the workers nicknamed 'slap-dash'. Apparently the bright new buttons became tarnished after only two weeks' wear, and the makers of the Florentine button again triumphed. In 1840 the metal-button makers made another trip to London and tried, unsuccessfully, to lobby Prince Albert. But, according to the *History and Description of the Great Exhibition*: 'The charm would not work twice, and you never see a gilt button now [1851] except upon the terribly high-collared coat of some devoted adherent to old fashions, nestling in the corner of the stage box on first nights.'

The Golden Age had died and was buried. From then to the end of the nineteenth century men's coats were trimmed with the covered Florentine button.

These buttons for outerwear, and linen buttons for underwear and household goods, were made by much the same method as that described in *Household Words* (1850):

> First rows of women sit, each at her machine, with the handle in her right hand, and a sheet of thin metal in the other. She punches out circles faster than the cook cuts pastry. By the same method, the rough pasteboard is cut out, and linen for shirt buttons; silk and satin, in short all the round parts of the button. Very young children gather up the cut circles. Little boys, 'just out of the cradle', range the pasteboard circles, and pack them close, on edge, in boxes or trays; and girls, as young, arrange on a table the linen circles. Meantime the machines are busy at work. Some are punching out the middle of the round bits of iron, or copper, or pasteboard, to allow the linen within to protrude, so as to be laid hold by the needle which is to sew the button. Another machine wraps the metal top of the button in cloth, turns downs the edges, fixes the pasteboard mould, and the prepared back, and closes all the rims, so as to complete the putting together of the five parts which compose the Florentine button.

An example of such a button is seen in black on the left of plate 11 (5th down).

It is not surprising that both the Florentine button and numerous variations had prominence at the 1851 Exhibition, some of the metal-button makers having accepted the inevitable. William Aston, Hardman & Illife of Newhall Street, and William Elliott & Sons were named in the Exhibition catalogue as showing Florentines, and other small manufacturers exhibited various similar types of cloth-covered buttons including many varieties of upholstery buttons. It is likely that some of them were merely engaged in assembling purchased components. William Aston employed 400 operatives at the time and the components used annually included 47,856 yards of Florentine lasting and 26,587½ yards of canvas. Until the introduction of machinery apparently one-third of the material was cut to waste, but by 1851 Aston had fifteen machines, which it was reported not only effected a great saving of material, but were automatic and worked well.

The official catalogue of the 1851 Exhibition lists Mr J. Aston as displaying silk, satin, velvet and linen buttons, but in *The History and Description of the Great Exhibition* favourable comment is made on velvet buttons shown by Mr *Ashton*: It is not known which name was correct, and it can only be guessed that one of these is the

---

Plate 10 shows a selection of Dorset thread buttons, once the property of Lady Dorothy Neville and now in a private collection in Somerset. The photograph is reproduced here by permission of the owners. (Dorset buttons are also shown in the centre of plate 11.)

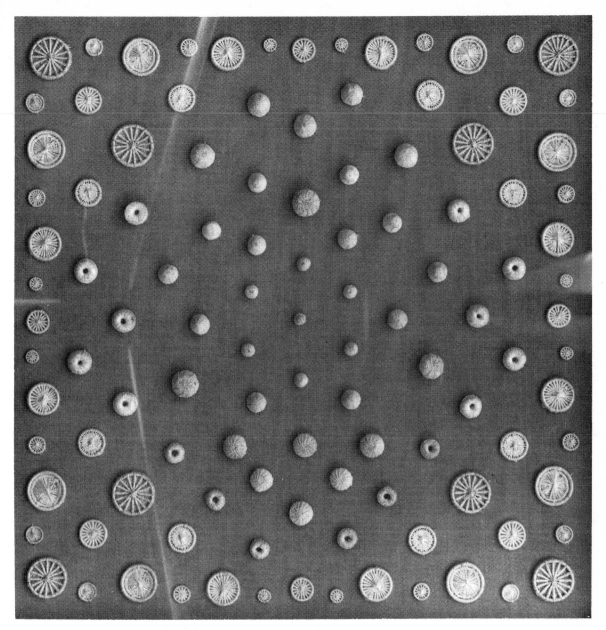

10 *Dorset thread buttons*

manufacturer blamed by Mr Case for ruining the Dorset industry (see Dorset thread buttons).

DORSET THREAD BUTTONS

These little buttons, which during the first part of the nineteenth century were found on the majority of underclothes and nightwear, have recently become a centre of attention and not a little romancing. A large number were transported to the United States with the object of selling them for charity, others were auctioned, and newspaper publicity has been given to people engaged in reviving the craft.

Many stories have circulated in the west of England about the Dorset buttons, and buttons have even been displayed by their owners as purporting to have been worn by Queen Victoria and other notables! The facts regarding the cottage industry of 'buttony', as it was known in Dorset, are set out in an article by Captain J. E. Acland in the *Dorset Natural History and Antiquarian Field Club Proceedings* (1914).

The majority of Dorset buttons are white, but small numbers of black and grey ones have been seen. There are two main types: those made by covering a small disk of sheep's horn with a piece of rag and then working over the whole with fine stitching, and those made by working with linen thread on a circle of wire.

The former, known as clothwork or high-top buttons, were first made at Shaftesbury during the eighteenth century and Abraham Case is reputed to have invented and popularized them. They were used on ladies' dresses, and were occasionally found in a flatter shape. The wire-ring type of button was developed there by a grandson of Abraham Case during the reign of George II, and at Bere Regis a relative organized button making of a similar kind. In 1758 Peter Case succeeded to the Bere Regis business and subsequently built Clayton Square, Liverpool, on the profits he made.

At the end of the eighteenth century a school for poor children was established at Milton Abbey by Lady Caroline Damer, and they were instructed in buttony and other crafts. By 1803 Milborne Stileham was the central depot for the buttons, and Peter Case junior was in charge; he was later succeeded by two nephews.

During the first half of the nineteenth century the business expanded rapidly and numerous depots were established throughout the country, to which the workers brought the buttons they made at home each week. A London office was organized and overseas agents were later appointed in Europe and North America. This satisfactory position continued until the Great Exhibition of 1851 when machine-made buttons made their appearance. Captain Acland quotes Mr Case as speaking of Ashton's patent machine button and the subsequent ruination of the Dorset industry because of these mass-produced linen buttons.

The Dorset people, not having other work to turn to, suffered badly, and the gentry of the county arranged for hundreds of them to be shipped to Australia and Canada where work prospects were better. By the beginning of the twentieth century only a handful of people, most of them connected with a charitable institution in Lytchett Minster near Poole, made thread buttons. In 1912 the sales of buttons amounted to

---

On plate 11, rows 1 and 2 show Leek buttons; below them is a circle of Dorset thread ones. French knobs are shown on each side, with examples of Florentine and thread-worked in black below on the left, and metal shell and fabric on the right. Velvet-backs and ribbon buttons are shown in the two bottom rows.

Background—blotting paper.

11 *Various fabric buttons*

£38 ($92), whereas a hundred years earlier they had been in the region of £12,000 ($2,880). Currently, Dorset buttons are produced as a gimmick by one or two enthusiasts in the Shaftesbury area, and displays of the old ones can be viewed at the Dorset County Museum in Dorchester, the Museum of Costume in Bath, and the Victoria & Albert Museum in London. It is interesting to note that at the 1851 Exhibition J. Fisher of Blandford, Dorset, is catalogued as exhibiting wire buttons. Unfortunately no other details are given, so it is not known if these were in fact Dorset buttons, or some other variety using wire. Blandford, today a market town, in mid-Victorian times had greater civic importance, and it was more frequently known by its full title of Blandford Forum.

Captain Acland gives an interesting description of the preparation of the wires for the flat buttons:

> The names of the wire buttons were mites, bird's eye, spangles, shirt, jams, waistcoats, and outsizes, and four different sized wires were used. The wires or rings were made from a roll of wire, burned and twisted on a spindle, the nipped ends put together and soldered by dipping in hot melted solder. This work was done by expert girls or boys called winders and dippers, and others called stringers counted the rings and threaded them in lots of 144. The brass wire was from Birmingham, brought in waggons with very wide wheels, a ton or ton and a half at a load.

After the buttons had been worked they were mounted on papers, different colours being used to denote different qualities. The people who did this work were known as paperers and could earn up to 9s ($1.10) a week, which was considered an excellent wage.

LEEK BUTTONS

At Leek in Staffordshire the local farming community produced handworked buttons during the first half of the nineteenth century. The name Leek button was subsequently applied also to similar thread buttons made in the midlands and north of England.

Traditionally Macclesfield silk was used for the buttons, and then production was a peasant craft as in Dorset. However, from the examples lent to me by Leek Public Library, it appears that the midlanders had greater artistic ability than their southern counterparts.

Black was the traditional colour for the buttons, which pre-dated the Florentine button for men's wear, but later a wide variety of colours and designs were used for waistcoat buttons. Those shown at the top of plate 11 include blues, reds and purples, as well as green, yellow and fawn. The curious barrel-shaped button is worked in deep-blue silk. The working was done with a needle over a wood or metal mould.

In 1842 a man named Isaac Moss patented what he called a Leek button, which he described as having a metal ring shell, which was sometimes covered with material. In 1848 an improvement was patented by Charles Rawley, who appears to have used metal shells, each with a hole in the centre for the passage of the needle. The shells were to be covered with silk twist or other material and then placed in dies where a back shell with a flexible shank was pressed into them and flattened. Whether or not this method of manufacture succeeded is unknown. At the time of the Great Exhibition, Charles Rowley of Newhall Street, Birmingham, is listed as a manufacturer. He produced chiefly military accessories, but mention is made of metal brace buttons of a type specifically designed to prevent the attaching thread being cut by the button eyelet hole. There was also a Mr S. A. Rowley, button manufacturer, who died in 1846; his business was bought by Green, Cadbury & Richards in 1876, when pearl buttons were the chief product and no mention is made of an association with either Charles or his inventions.

I have not seen any examples of buttons from Rawley, Leek, but two examples of thread-worked buttons with flexible shanks are shown in black on the left of plate 11 immediately below, but not easily distinguishable from, the Florentine one. Examples of the traditional type can be seen on waistcoats at the Museum of Costume in Bath. On the right of plate 11 are three examples of fabric buttons with a metal edging. These date from the early twentieth century and were made in Austria or Germany. The fabric is machine-woven.

A similar type of needle-woven button, using a flat wood or card disc, was made in the Dundee area of Scotland at the beginning of this century. Examples made by a Mrs Moffatt, her mother and grandmother, were purchased by me during 1969 and photographs of them were shown in *Just Buttons* for July of that year. In her comments on them the editor mentions that most varieties of thread button can be cleaned by being stirred in a jar of dry-cleaning fluid and then laid to dry outside.

OTHER FABRIC BUTTONS

French knobs. Little is known about these buttons, shown on plate 11. The cards on which the four shown here were originally mounted indicate that they are French. A dealer friend who has visited France regularly tells me they are hand-crocheted over wood moulds. They are reputed to have been worn by nineteenth-century Parisian prostitutes who attached long lines of them to their blouses: the waggling of the buttons was intended to attract the attention of potential customers.

Velvet backs (2nd row from bottom, plate 11). An American collector term for two-piece metal buttons incorporating velvet instead of woven silk or other fabric. They were made in quite large numbers from 1880 onwards, but as can be seen by the centre example, deteriorate rapidly in wear. The earliest example shown is in the centre of the bottom row, which is trimmed with woven ribbon and velvet. This dates from the late 1880s.

Ribbon buttons. The city of Coventry in Warwickshire became famous during the nineteenth century for woven ribbon. Joseph Marie Jaquard had invented in 1801 what became known later as the Jaquard loom, which was brought from France to Coventry and gradually became almost universal. At first the British workers resented it and the idea of working in organised factories instead of having looms in their own homes. Riots occurred in Coventry, one factory was burnt to the ground, and the troops had to be called in to settle matters. However by the time of the 1851 Exhibition the ribbon trade was flourishing and Coventry put on a grand display. Ten years later a slump had hit the trade, and although ribbons were shown at the 1862 Exhibition, manufacturers were turning to the production of woven pictures, bookmarks etc in order to keep their operatives employed.

One such firm which had received high praise at the 1862 Exhibition was J. & J. Cash. Cash's, known to every British schoolchild as the maker of the name tapes sewn on school clothing, was founded by brothers John and Joseph, and is still under the direction of descendants. The present managing director, Mr J. L. M. Graham, confirmed that the covers for the small black and white buttons at the bottom of plate 11 were probably made by his company, incorporated with the actual buttons elsewhere, and then distributed by Cash's.

He also gave me the Union Jack buttons shown on the frontispiece and with the commemorative buttons on plate 35. Unfortunately many of the firm's records were destroyed when Coventry was blitzed during World War II. The Union Jack buttons were made originally for the coronation of King George VI in 1937, and the others were probably earlier productions dating from the late 1920s. Mrs Sally Luscomb mentions similar buttons in *The Collectors Encyclopædia of Buttons*.

LINEN BUTTONS

Numerous firms made linen buttons during the latter part of the nineteenth century, following the invention of various types of machines for covering them. At the 1851 Exhibition, William Aston, Hardman & Illife, William Elliott & Sons, J. Catwin & Sons, Great Charles Street, and J. Aston, St Pauls Square, Birmingham, all showed what were known as patent linen buttons. Many linen-button makers have continued production until the present day, and in 1876 a well-known firm, Green, Cadbury & Richards, went to great lengths to advertise its wares. A booklet was produced extolling the goods, and 158,000 pattern cards, each containing souvenir samples of white linen buttons in ten sizes, were sent to lady residents of London. This venture cost the firm £329 ($790) in postage alone. At this time the company was employing 400 operatives and producing between 10,000 and 15,000 gross buttons per week (not all linen ones).

Green, Cadbury & Richards produced a linen button named the Very button, and in 1876 issued a notice threatening legal action against those who imitated it. Also in that year the firm effected the take-over of a pearl-button business belonging to Mr S. A. Rowley, but managed by Joseph Anstey since Rowley's death in 1846. The Very button and Green, Cadbury & Richards' other products were evidently well received in London: various magazines, including *Once a Week, Family Herald, The Young Englishwoman* and *Cassell's Household Guide* commented favourably on them.

Mr Richards visited the Vienna Exhibition in 1873 and on his return published a report. He did not think much of the linen buttons he had seen:

> France is represented in this class by Parent and Co. of Paris, with a few elaborately made half ball buttons in best white cloth, rather illustrating what can be made than what are made, and in regular demand. A few German makers show examples of flat eyeletted linen buttons, wretchedly finished. They have not made any advance since 1867. Birmingham in this speciality stands pre-eminent for excellence and cheapness, the same remark applies to Florentine buttons.

A firm which was very well known at the beginning of this century for the production of linen and other buttons, and which is still in business under another name, was Buttons Ltd. This company was formed in 1907 as an amalgamation of several nineteenth-century firms, including the descendants of Green, Cadbury & Richards. Trademarks include the Three Domes, a Crowing Cock, a Horse Head, a Swan, a Fleur-de-lis, a Unicorn, and perhaps the best known, the Crossed Swords.

The company made large quantities of all types of button until World War I, when it concentrated on military goods. After World War II the company diversified and button production was, and still is, largely confined to metals. The company is now known as Francis Sumner Engineering Ltd. The present managing director, Mr W. J. Flückiger, kindly lent me an old catalogue dating from the early days of Buttons Ltd. It is the only one still in existence and a work of art! Leather-bound and embossed, it contains illustrations of over forty different types of linen buttons, together with sets for display, cabinets for storage etc.

Plate 12 shows a section from one of the old sample cards of James Grove & Sons, and is reproduced with their permission. (A sample of glass buttons made by the company is shown on the top row of plate 26.)

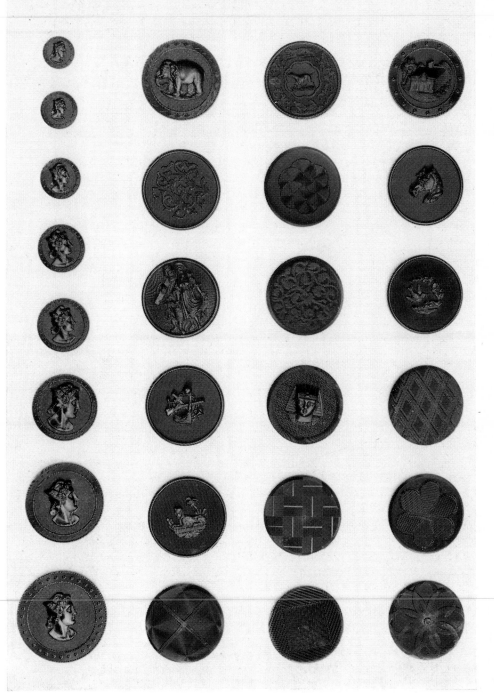

12 *A sample card of horn buttons*

The buttons are much the same as any linen buttons of the period, but the cards on which they were mounted for sale are quite intriguing. Brightly coloured and decorated in the manner of old cigarette packets, they illustrate hands of cards, ivy plants, gramophone horns, artist's palettes, etc. Some open out to show varieties of buttons, others were made to store in boxes. The Very button is shown on a blue and gold ground with the Unicorn trade mark and other items include penny cards of twenty-four brace buttons and vegetable-ivory buttons by the gross.

The Horn-Button Makers of Halesowen

The story of the Halesowen (Worcestershire) button makers is the story of one determined man's fight against adversity. This man was James Grove.

There is archaeological evidence that horn buttons were made in the Halesowen area as early as 1750, but commercial production was pioneered in 1840 by a Mr William Harris and his brother Thomas. These men were devout Methodists with a keen interest in landscape gardening, and given to eating breakfast under the apple trees at their Springhill works before commencing the day's business with a prayer meeting. The workers were encouraged to attend church, neatly and correctly attired; no doubt partly motivated by the presence of the bosses in the family pew!

James Grove began work as an apprentice to Thomas Harris, and made such rapid progress that when Harris went away to start a works at Frankley, and his son proved inefficient as manager of Halesowen, Grove was asked to take over, on a profit-sharing basis. Grove accepted this proposition and the works flourished. However, when Harris senior returned for the day of reckoning, it seems that he so far forgot his Methodist principles as to default on payment! Grove left, and at once set up in business independently, taking with him as a partner a man named Dalton. Unfortunately Dalton wasted his substance with riotous living and the partnership was dissolved, Grove receiving financial assistance from a kind brother. In 1860, three years after commencement, the firm acquired its own transport in the form of a horse and trap, and journeys to Birmingham were found to be profitable. Subsequent immediate expansion was a direct

---

Plate 13 shows a selection of processed horn buttons, together with one or two made in composition to imitate horn. Processed horn buttons can be distinguished from composition by the 'prick mark' at the back, made by the needle-like tool used to lift them from the mould. In the bottom row are seen, left to right, a sawn section of horn and two natural horn buttons, before and after polishing (James Grove), a cottage-industry self-shanked button from the north of England, and an old natural horn button excavated in a Somerset garden.

The button on the left in row 2 is marked 'Fins, Paris'. In row 3, the 1st shows a municipal coat of arms, and is unmarked, the 2nd is backmarked 'Depose. Paris F.C.', the 3rd is a City of London Police button, one of those used to replace metal buttons during the blackout in World War II (unmarked). In row 4, the 1st is backmarked 'Boyd Cooper. Reg. 70795, 4 George St. Hanover Sq. W.I.', the 2nd is an Automobile Association (the largest British motoring organisation) button, the 3rd is from the St John Ambulance Brigade. In the 5th row, the 1st is Royal Irish Constabulary, 'ensign make', the 2nd, with Merchant Navy design, is backmarked 'Kenning London'. In the 6th row, centre, the GPO (General Post Office) button is backmarked 'James Grove'.

The other buttons are unmarked.

Background—leather.

13 *Processed and natural horn buttons*

result of large orders for horn buttons for both Federal and Confederate armies in the American Civil War.

Grove's original premises were rented from his father-in-law, a spade maker, but in 1867, after various abortive attempts, a plot of land suitable for the new factory was acquired. About this time several employees joined the firm who were to remain for their entire working lives, the most notable being a woman named Maria Florence, who produced twenty-two children and worked until she was eighty years of age.

After the American Civil War, depression hit the horn-button trade, and Grove became worried and disheartened. However, an unexpected order from New York for £300 ($720) worth of buttons caused much excitement, and everyone set to work to produce the goods, which were despatched promptly: the firm is still awaiting payment! But Groves was not the type of man to be put off by impending bankruptcy, and took the horse and trap to Birmingham where he investigated other methods of button making. As a result he hired a retired trapeze artist with a knowledge of glass-button manufacture and, together with a second-hand four-horse-powered table engine, they went to work.

His next venture was the production of dyed horn ornaments and brooches, which sold well as imitation jet. In 1870 a French political exile arrived in the district and found work with Grove. In 1873 the importation of buffalo horn from South America, coupled with the adoption of French methods of manufacture, resulted in almost total reorganisation of the works, and great expansion in the export market. Due to increased tariffs the French export business collapsed in 1875; but again, being a man of determination, Grove set up a plant to produce vegetable-ivory buttons from corozo nuts and, until the price of nuts became inflated, he found this profitable.

All the while horn buttons were being produced and new improved methods patented, as James Grove never allowed himself to become totally sidetracked from the firm's original product. The company of James Grove & Sons was formed in 1882, when he took his two sons, George and Arthur, into partnership. Like a true Victorian father he underpaid them. He died in 1886 aged sixty-two, leaving behind him the only prosperous horn business in the district, and a flourishing township at Hawne, where there had previously been only a small village adjoining Halesowen.

In 1971 a screaming motorway connects Halesowen with Birmingham, and the directors of Groves jet to and fro across the Atlantic. But much of the old factory remains. There is still a garden, with apple trees, and the old buildings of soft warm brick and stone have been adapted to modern production methods. Groves are busy producing buttons by the million, many of plastic substances, but the descendants of James Grove carry on the family tradition and make horn buttons to meet the current fashion for natural fabrics and materials.

MAKING HORN BUTTONS

Before 1873 all horn buttons were made from processed horn, known to Americans as plastic horn because of its plasticity when heated. Moulded horn is another term used to describe this type of button. The *History and Description of the Great Exhibition* describes how such buttons were made:

All the buttons on plate 14 are of excellent quality, and they show a wide variety of techniques and finishes.
Background—Viyella, design by Liberty's of London.

38

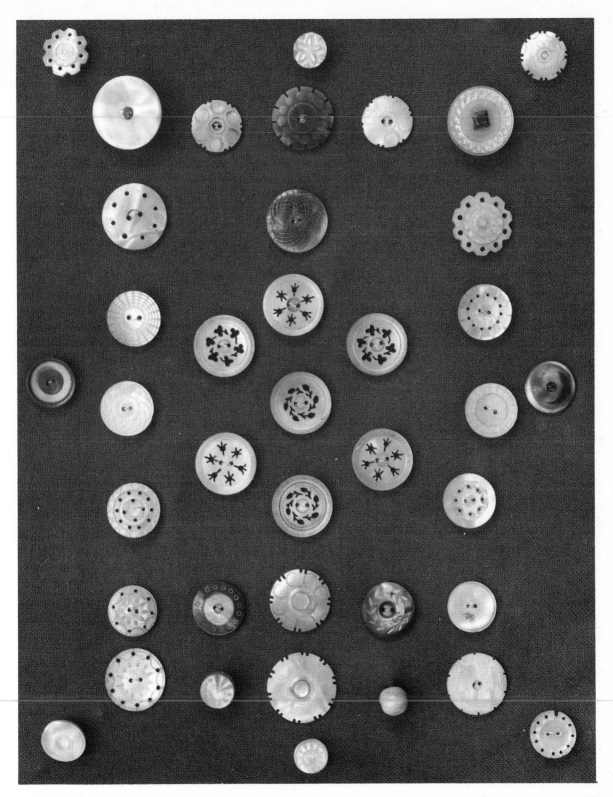

14 *Pearl buttons*

Horn buttons are made from the hoofs of horned cattle; those of horses are not suitable for the purpose. The hoofs are boiled until soft, and cut into halves; then blanks are cut out. These are placed in vats containing a strong dye, red, green or black, and a shank is then fixed in. The button is then placed in a mould where the under surface is stamped with the maker's name. A dozen moulds are put into an iron box, and heated over an oven until the horn is as soft as wax, and then an upper mould with the pattern for the top of the button is pressed down, fitting close to the lower mould. The moulds having been placed in the press, and submitted to its action, the buttons are complete except that the rough edges require paring. Brushes worked by steam then run over and polish the buttons, and they are ready for the sorter.

A Mr Wells is noted as exhibiting some horn buttons of considerable merit, and Messrs Ingram 'illustrate very fully the horn button in its history and varieties'.

Birmingham Museum has examples of this type of button on display, including a stamped horn button marked 'Cox', examples of sporting buttons in black horn, and an undyed button marked 'Cox and Ingram 1835'. Tom Cox took out a patent in 1854 for horn buttons and a large four-hole button with rope border and sporting motif is included in the display. James Grove is represented by a natural button with a self-shank and bearing the royal coat of arms.

After the 1873 importation of buffalo horn, the making of natural horn buttons became popular, and this is the method used by James Grove & Sons today. The horns are stored in a large yard at the side of the factory, and when brought in they first of all have the solid tips removed for making duffle-type buttons and then the rest of the horn is either sawn into slices or opened, flattened and cut into blanks. Preliminary matching then takes place, before the fronts and backs are turned on automatic machines. Preliminary polishing follows, then hole drilling and countersinking on both sides in one operation. Finally the buttons are smooth polished by tumbling, sorted for colour match and attached to cards with adhesive tape.

Pearl Buttons

Under the foundations of Birmingham Town Hall are many tons of mollusc shell, mainly of the variety Pentadinae. During the nineteenth century they were the raw material for over 2,000 pearl button makers. There is a story told in Birmingham that when a world shortage of the shell occurred in the 1870s serious consideration was given to a plan to demolish the Town Hall in order to obtain the buried shells. The profit was to have been used to build a new civic centre. In 1971 a new civic centre is under construction, but not from the proceeds of button making!

Many firms were engaged in the production of pearl buttons in Birmingham during the nineteenth century. In 1850 an article in *Household Words* commented:

> Birmingham supplied almost the whole world. A very few pearl buttons were made in Sheffield; and that was all. In the United States where the merchants could get almost any quantity of the shell, from their trade with Manilla and Singapore, the buttons were not made. The Americans bought an incredible quantity from Birmingham.

The majority of the buttons on plate 15 are early and mid-nineteenth-century productions and include several 'black' pearls. The two buttons at the bottom corners were purchased in the Republic of Ireland, and are possibly of Dublin manufacture. The others are British and French. The button at the left in the 5th row is similar to one in the Luckock collection (qv). The others show various techniques and finishes, including engraving, steel trim (lower centre), gold leaf (two floral designs on white), and pearl inlaid in resin (horse-shoe).

Background—felt.

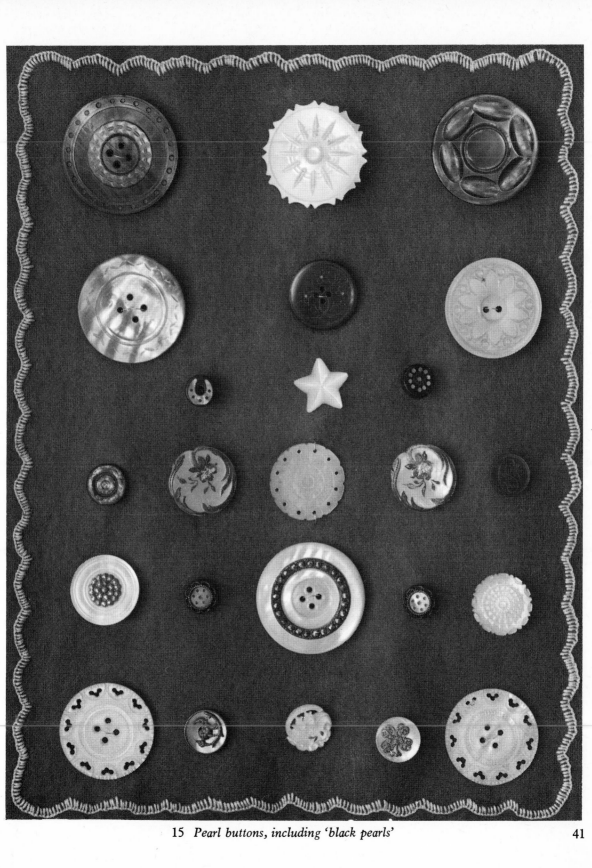

15 *Pearl buttons, including 'black pearls'*

In the *History of the Great Exhibition*, Mr Banks, Messrs Elliott and Mr Brissrabb were mentioned as exhibiting pearl buttons. The Brissrabb display included buttons of 'black' pearl; these were made from the darker areas of the shell which had earlier been discarded as unsuitable material. Messrs Elliott were quoted as producing buttons with metal rims, and this in 1851 was considered a novel idea. The first mentioned contributor, Mr Banks, was at that time trading in Newhall Street, where he had been since 1841. In 1855 he joined up with a Mr Hammond, who had previously made metal buttons. The business was then conducted from the Parade, but later moved to St Paul's Square where it remained until it was either closed or taken over in 1923. The pearl buttons shown on plate 14 are all reputed to have been made by the firm of Banks & Hammond.

On 19 April 1838 at Eccleston in Staffordshire, Samuel Turner was married to Catherine Leent, daughter of Leent the Birmingham wholesaler. Subsequently they had ten children, the ninth of whom was named Arthur. Samuel Turner became a button manufacturer and had premises in Northampton Street, Birmingham. According to his descendants he died at a fairly early age of a broken heart caused by misdeeds of his eldest son, who had departed to America with the family cash box and its contents. The business was closed. Arthur joined Banks & Hammond in St Paul's Square and remained in their employ until his retirement in 1915.

Arthur Turner was married to a Miss Sheldon, descendant of the Ralph Sheldon who in 1569 had brought the art of making tapestry to England. On the occasion of this wedding, special pearl buttons were handmade for the bridal gown. Seven of these, together with the others shown on plate 14, were purchased from one of Arthur's daughters, now an elderly lady. The bridal buttons are the seven in the centre of the plate.

MAKING PEARL BUTTONS

The shells for pearl-button making were brought to London from various areas of the Pacific and Indian oceans. They arrived in mahogany crates and after unpacking and inspection were auctioned in the Mincing Lane salerooms and elsewhere. They were then transported to Birmingham by road or rail where merchants re-sorted them, sending the coarser shells on to Sheffield to be sold to knife-handle makers.

The shells were then taken to the factories where they were washed and cut into blanks. This was done with a tubular saw mounted on a lathe. In the 1850s and earlier the machine was worked by hand, but was later powered. After cutting, the tubes of shell were split into sections and a small boy was employed to rasp the blanks on one side, so that when they were subsequently placed in a lathe they would lie flat. The turner then took over and it was at this stage the buttons were given their shape and decoration. Engraving and fine decorating were done by specialists.

The prepared blanks were then sorted into lots, according to the fastening method chosen, and either drilled through or partially drilled prior to shank fixing. Engraved or finely decorated buttons were normally partly drilled, and a wedge-shaped hole was

---

Plate 16 shows a selection of buttons with metal trimmings, dating from the 1850s. The two small ones near the centre are of abalone shell; some of the others show the use of cut steel (either end of 2nd row), brass (top row), spelter (bottom corners), pewter and tin.

Background—quilting on satin from a nineteenth-century wedding gown.

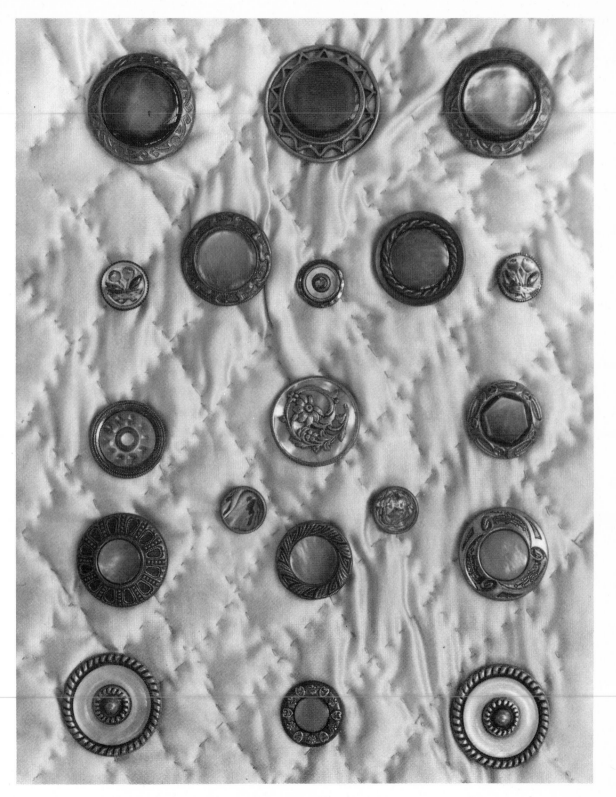

16　*Buttons with metal trimmings*　　　　43

made into which a loop shank with two small prongs was inserted. The shank was then hit firmly with a hammer causing the prongs to spread and make a secure fastening. The *Illustrated Exhibitor* 1852 notes that a button shanked by this method was capable of supporting half a hundredweight (56lb)!

The buttons were then polished with brushes, soap and rotten stone (a powdered limestone) by women employees. Female labour was also used for the drilling of the sew-through buttons. The final treatment was the cording or milling of the edges. The carding of the buttons was often done by out-workers, who used foil packing paper or bright blue paper. *Household Words* 1850 describes such an out-worker:

> We saw a woman in her own home surrounded by her children, tacking the buttons on their stiff paper for sale. There was not much foil in this case, but a brilliant blue paper, which looked as well. This woman sews forty gross in a day. She could formerly by excessive diligence, sew fifty or sixty gross, but forty is her number now, and a large number it is considering that each button has to be picked up from a heap, ranged in its row and tacked with two stitches.

Another contemporary source tells of little children being used to position the buttons for factory workers to sew. Earnings at this time varied between 10s and 15s per week ($1.20 - $1.90).

Pearl-button making was introduced into the USA in 1885, using shells from China, and later from Australia, Ceylon and the South Seas. By the beginning of the twentieth century many manufacturers were also using abalone shells from the Californian coast, and buttons made from these shells with their beautiful rainbow colourings are regarded with special affection by present-day American collectors. Freshwater shells, nicknamed niggerheads, were gathered from the Mississippi, and between 1890 and 1900 accounted for almost half the total output of button manufacture.

One of the leading firms of pearl-button makers in America was B. Schwanda & Sons of New York and Connecticut. Benedict Schwanda, who had commenced button making in Czechoslovakia, emigrated to America in 1892 and opened a business as button maker and importer. He was joined by two sons at the beginning of the century and the business expanded rapidly. During the 1940s this firm arranged displays of its wares for the benefit of button collectors and gave writers and others conducted tours of the works.

In December 1969, *Just Buttons* carried a very sad account of the liquidation sale of the company. The stock and machinery were auctioned off in lots for cash. Government officials from the department of taxes attended in person! It appears that the directors had allowed their love of the old and beautiful to override the need for sound economics. By refusing to incorporate the production of plastic buttons into their programme they had bankrupted themselves. A very sad state of affairs, but regrettably there is no room for sentiment in industry. A direct contrast to this can be seen in the fortunes of the English Glass Company at Leicester, where some of the directors, also of Czechoslovakian origin, realised that however much they personally may appreciate beauty, the factory must be a viable concern.

The Luckock Collection

This collection of buttons is housed in the Birmingham Museum. Many of the buttons

---

Plate 17 shows a small selection of buttons from the collection, and is reproduced by permission of the City of Birmingham Museum.

17 *Buttons from the Luckock Collection*   45

in it are of earlier date than those covered by this book, but are worth consideration as they represent an unsolved mystery.

The buttons were left to the museum under the will of a Miss Ruddle who died in the Isle of Wight during the 1940s. They were mislaid and subsequently 'discovered' in the early 1950s. An account of the discovery and the deciphering of the accompanying documents was written by Adrian Oswald and Faith Russell Smith and published in *The Connoisseur* in September 1954. They had spent some time trying to discover the history of the buttons, but apparently were not able to find out how Miss Ruddle came to possess them and why she left them to the museum. Since July 1970, assisted by another member of the museum staff, I have been investigating the history of the buttons, but have made limited progress. Letters to many people in the Isle of Wight have produced the information that Miss Ruddle was the daughter of a Unitarian minister at Newport, who pre-deceased her. None of the many people consulted know of any living relative and few remember the lady herself. Miss Ruddle is reputed to have been a descendant of the Nettlefold and Chamberlain families of Birmingham but how she came by the buttons is still a mystery.*

According to the documents accompanying the buttons, they purport to be a collection manufactured in Birmingham principally for foreign courts. The collection was apparently assembled by James Luckock of Birmingham between the years 1844-9, but some buttons were obviously added later. Many of them were made long before that date, and indeed inspection suggests the mid-eighteenth century as the date of manufacture for the majority. While it is known that Birmingham was responsible for many fine examples of workmanship, including those demonstrated in the collection, I personally would attribute some of them to continental sources.

James Luckock was born in 1781. After an apprenticeship in the plating business, he tried his hand, unsuccessfully, at buckle making in partnership with his brother. Subsequently he ran the jewellery branch of a manufacturing business belonging to Samuel Pemberton. Later he opened his own business as a button maker and jeweller in St Paul's Square—he may in fact have made some of the buttons in the collection. In 1787 he was one of a group of people who started the first Sunday School in Birmingham, and in 1817 wrote a book for use there. He died in 1835.

The Luckock collection is well worth a visit as it contains some superb examples of button making. It is hoped that more information about it will be available shortly.

* It has now been discovered that Miss Ruddle was James Luckock's great-grand-daughter.

TWO:
THE PLATEAU 1876-1910

Vegetable Ivory

Vegetable ivory is the trade name for the kernel of the corozo nut, which grows on a palm found in South America and Africa. In its natural state it looks like a small coconut. After the very hard outer shell has been removed, the white kernel, which resembles animal ivory, can be easily turned or cut. Trinkets made from entire nuts are frequently seen in antique and junk shops; they were a popular tourist item at the end of the nineteenth century.

The button industry appears to have discovered the potential of the nut during the 1850s, and at the Paris Exhibition of 1862 a display from British firms was shown. However it was not until well into the 1870s that mass production of nut buttons commenced. Vegetable-ivory buttons quickly replaced bone buttons, and consequently the price of nuts became inflated. This caused some teething troubles, as we have seen in the Grove story (page 36), but nationally mass production continued until the turn of the century when the discovery of celluloid for button making started a gradual decline in the use of the corozo nut, which was accelerated by the introduction of other plastic materials.

By the beginning of World War II production in Britain had virtually ceased, but it is interesting to note that as late as 1945 Imperial Chemical Industries issued a technical circular dealing with the dyeing of vegetable-ivory buttons. Limited production is still carried on in Italy and Spain, the former having been a major producer of such buttons. Apparently the Spanish use the nuts as ballast for ships coming from South America. In America, vegetable-ivory buttons were produced in Leeds, Massachusetts, from 1864. Later Rochester, New York, became the centre of the trade.

MAKING VEGETABLE-IVORY BUTTONS

The hard outer shell was removed and the kernel of the nut was cut into slices and then cured in a kiln to prevent warping. After machine sorting, button blanks were cut with tubular saws in the same way as for pearl buttons. Softening by heat followed, and then the carving of designs and hole drilling. Shank insertion was carried out where required and then buttons were soaked to open the pores of the material prior to dyeing.

For single-colour buttons dyeing was done by a dipping process. For those where a two-tone or multi-colour finish was required a stencil process was used. After the dye had been 'fixed' in vats the buttons were polished by tumbling, and finally sorted and attached to cards. Alternative treatments included embossing by hand or machine, leaving a section of the rind on the nut, or using nuts in conjunction with other materials.

It appears that all manufacturers had trouble with the dyeing process. Several writers mention this as being one of the disadvantages of production, and one that the pioneers of plastics made much of. In their 1945 leaflet Imperial Chemical Industries advocated the use of durafur dyestuffs, which they maintained would produce a good level of dye

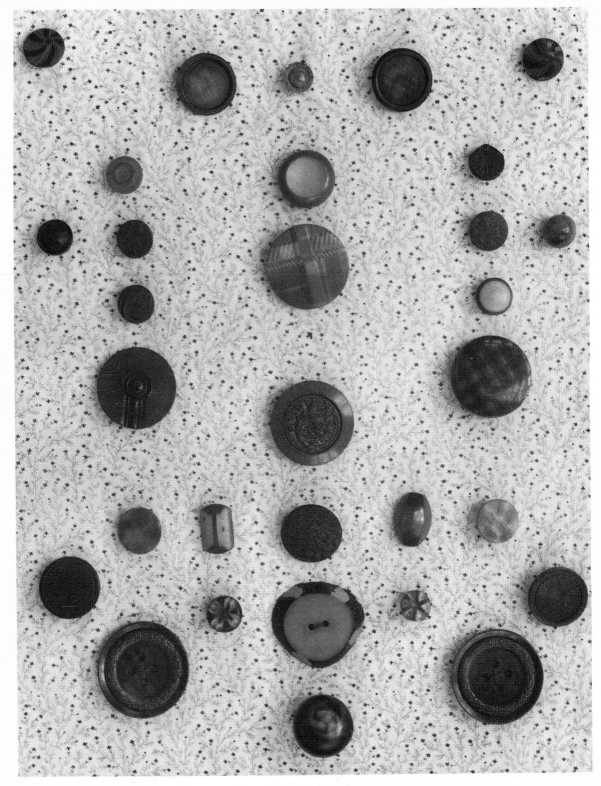

18 *Vegetable-ivory buttons*

and solidity of shade. Apparently buttons dyed with vegetable dyes had subsequently faded and otherwise deteriorated during storage. One of the reasons given for this was that as the nut kernel is marked in growth rings, as is a tree, the dye was not absorbed evenly.

Vegetable-ivory buttons were always considered 'cheap' in much the same way as some plastic types are now. Although many designs were charming and attractive in their mint state they could never be considered as high-fashion items. They deteriorated rapidly in wear, particularly when subjected to heavy-handed washerwomen, and bright sunlight often caused them to fade and split.

The Big Myth—Black 'Jet'

Twice daily I try to explain to would-be vendors of black buttons the difference between glass and jet; 99.9 per cent of the buttons supposed by their owners to be jet are in fact glass. I have never seen a real jet button, but examples do exist. Mrs Luscomb has one or two, and other examples have been authenticated in American collections. There are also some in a museum at Whitby in Yorkshire.

During the latter half of the nineteenth century very limited quantities of jet buttons were probably made in Yorkshire. But large quantities of jet ornaments were produced and also many items in a variety of materials to imitate jet; dyed horn was used by James Grove, for example (plate 12). True jet is a soft, black, coal-like substance, geologically known as lignite, and it has been a popular material for making ornaments since the Bronze Age. The best quality was found at Whitby, Yorkshire, but is now practically exhausted. Poorer qualities are found in Spain and France.

True jet is soft and light in weight, and finished articles resemble black sealing wax, but due to its tendency to chip and flake, jet is not very suitable for button making. Among the materials used to imitate it—Pennsylvania anthracite, coal, chalcedony stained black, and black glass—glass was the most satisfactory. It is much heavier than jet and can of course be worked in a liquid state. The origins of the jet-button myth rest solely with the manufacturers, who made black glass buttons and called them jet glass or imitation jet, referring to the colour and not the material. In time the words 'glass' and 'imitation' were omitted in use.

Pressed-glass buttons, especially black ones, were very fashionable from 1870 to 1910, and widows and elderly people continued to wear them until 1940. My grandmother, in common with thousands of others, transferred them from one garment to another until her death in the 1950s. She disliked and mistrusted plastic!

The majority of black glass buttons, like those on plate 19, were made in Bohemia (later Czechoslovakia), but some also in France, Germany and Austria. In America they were developed independently and produced in many east-coast locations.

Collectors who are in any doubt about the material from which such buttons are made should first of all inspect the backs. Glass in its molten state can be poured. Often one can see where the glass has been poured into the mould and around the shank. Glass is also harder than jet and, when knocked, it tends to splinter rather than chip.

Plate 18 shows a selection of vegetable-ivory buttons. The centre button has a metal inset. The stencil technique is shown on the plaid designs; the rind has been left on the button lower centre, and on either side of this are small spherical carved buttons.

Background—nineteenth-century calico print.

19 *Black pressed-glass buttons*

The making of the moulds for pressed-glass buttons required a great deal of skill. Close examination shows how many of the buttons not only depict flowers, birds etc, but also imitate the patterning of the fabrics on which they were to be sewn. The fifth button in the third row of plate 19 demonstrates this well: its centre represents watered silk.

Because of their abundance black glass buttons have been underrated by American collectors, which is a pity. Personally I find them more attractive than many of the metal picture types (plate 30) which are so avidly collected. The larger black glass buttons always have a market, even if a slow one, but the small ones as shown on plate 27 were made in such quantities that they are virtually unsaleable as collector items at present.

Lustre Glass

Not everyone wanted to wear black even in late Victorian times, and lustre-trimmed buttons were a popular alternative. These are the buttons which are frequently thought by the uninformed to be steel (qv) and which were originally made to imitate steel.

Lustre-glass buttons, shown in plate 20, can be found in almost all the patterns that were used for the black buttons, and are in fact made of glass dipped in lustre. Silver is the most popular colour, but gold is commonly seen, and there are also buttons trimmed with lustre as shown in plate 21.

Like the black buttons, the lustre ones are mainly of European origin. Unlike the black ones, they have been revived since World War II and can be found currently on sale in haberdasheries. New lustre buttons may be distinguished from old ones in several ways. The shank at the back on the new ones is frequently of the self-shank or built-up type. The old ones normally have metal shanks, two- or four-way inset for the larger buttons, or loop for the smaller ones. New buttons are thicker and heavier than old ones of the same size. The patterning on new ones is often coarser than that on the old.

Lustre trim rubs away in wear and like other types of old button this one does not take kindly to modern detergents or dry-cleaning fluids. Such buttons should be removed from garments before laundering or cleaning, and it should be remembered that they are damaged as easily as any other glass item.

Old pressed-glass buttons are frequently found in a very dirty condition. Washing in clear water removes surface dust, but to remove ingrained grime they should be brushed with a jeweller's silver brush or old toothbrush (bristle, not nylon). The black ones are not affected by soap or detergents, but lustre glass should be treated carefully with pure soap only. After brushing they should be rinsed in plenty of clear water and left to dry naturally on a cloth or blotting paper. If in a hurry a hair-dryer or fan heater can be used to hasten the drying process. Glass fractures if subjected to sudden changes of temperature, so very hot or cold water and direct heat should be avoided.

Clear Pressed Glass and Lacy Glass

The technique of pressing glass was developed by the Americans during the 1840s and subsequently used all over the world. It is suitable for any object of simple basic shape which can be taken from a mould like a pudding; molten glass is poured or dropped into the mould and a plunger then descends pressing the glass against the mould, and forming the inner or base surface itself.

Some of the finest examples of pressed glass are of American origin, and one of the

Plate 19 shows a selection of black pressed-glass buttons.
Background—velvet.

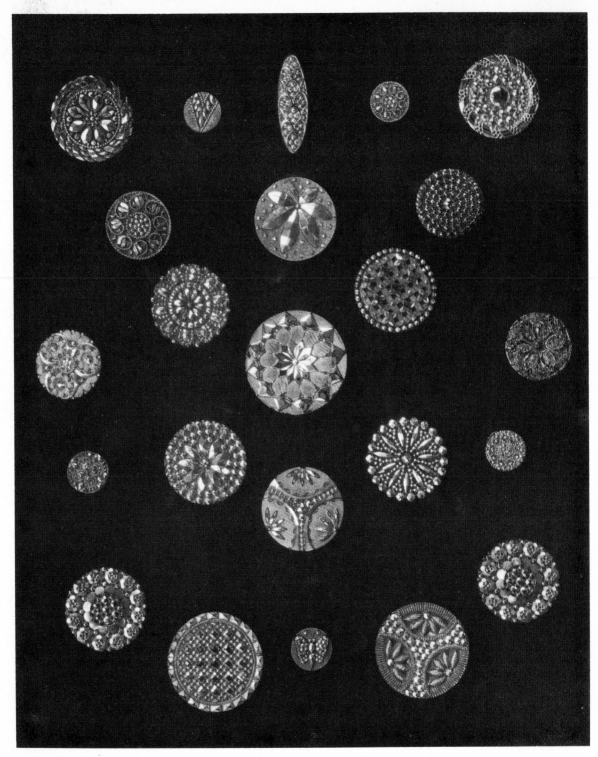

Plate 20 shows a selection of pressed-glass buttons finished with silver lustre. Background—velvet.

Plate 21 shows pressed-glass buttons, some with gold or silver lustre decoration. The paisley design (2nd row, centre) is a good example of gold decoration; the catherine wheel (1st left, 4th row) shows silver lustre decoration used to imitate steel.
Background—embroidered net, c 1910.

leading producers of it at the end of the nineteenth century was the Sandwich Glass Company of Boston. This company, which ceased operations in 1888, was responsible for many of the attractive items now known to collectors as lacy glass, so called from its lace-like patterning and appearance. The term lacy glass was also given by collectors to buttons originally supposed to have been made by the Sandwich Glass Company, but which have since proved to have originated in Austria and Bohemia. However, the classification has persisted. The discovery of these buttons in Britain helps to confirm that the original supposition was incorrect, for, so far as is known, the British have never imported glass buttons from America. These buttons were thin, and of clear pressed glass, sometimes with lustre trim but always with a coated back: the back was first coated with silver or gold lustre, and usually also given a protective coating of black paint. Lacy glass buttons have only been found in the two sizes shown on plate 22.

During wear the backing paint was easily damaged. American dealers used to strip the backing from the buttons in order to make them appear more like other lacy glass items and to support the theory that they came from Sandwich. Collectors therefore are primarily interested in good examples in mint or near-mint condition and, as these are relatively scarce, pay well for them. One current publication estimates the value of a mint button as four times that of a stripped one. Moral—it does not pay to strip!

Glass-Ball Buttons

The endless varieties of glass-ball buttons could well become a collection of themselves. They form one of the most beautiful 'groupings' (a term used by American collectors for types of button). It is not only the modern collector who is fascinated by them, for the *History and Description of the Great Exhibition* has this to say on the subject:

> We must not forget glass buttons, with which it was lately the pleasure of admiring mothers to sprinkle their little boys very profusely, and which are also much in demand for exportation to the African chiefs, who have the true barbarian love of glitter. There are two sorts, round and knob shaped. The former are made of sheet glass in various colours, and coated with lead, which is cut by hand into small squares, the corners of which are rounded with scissors, and the edges are ground on a wheel. The shank is then fastened; it is joined to a round piece of zinc the size of the button, and soldered to it. The knob buttons are made in a mould, a long rod of glass being softened in a furnace and clasped in the mould in which the shank has previously been fitted.

The human race has always been fascinated by coloured glass, and when I toured America in 1970 selling old buttons, I was only continuing a practice begun by my forefathers over 400 years ago!

The glass-ball buttons shown on plate 23 represent a selection dating from 1880 to 1910, and a wide variety of decoration. Many of them are made in the same way as glass marbles, and some of them are of Bohemian origin. In Bohemia (later Czechoslovakia) the making of such buttons was a cottage industry, with small glass-workers' establishments dotted about the rural areas. Visitors tell of the coloured glass rods

---

With the lacy glass buttons in plate 22 are examples of pressed glass made from 1880 to 1920. They include two in deep-amethyst glass with iridescent finish (top corners) and a deep-green button with gold trim (top centre). In row 2 are examples of Lalique-type glass, and in the centre of row 3 is a small amber glass button with silver trim. The Art Nouveau (qv) influence can be clearly seen in the fuchsia design of the matt-finished button on the right-hand side, 6th row. The three small ball buttons are not pressed glass, but were added for decorative purposes.
Background—velvet.

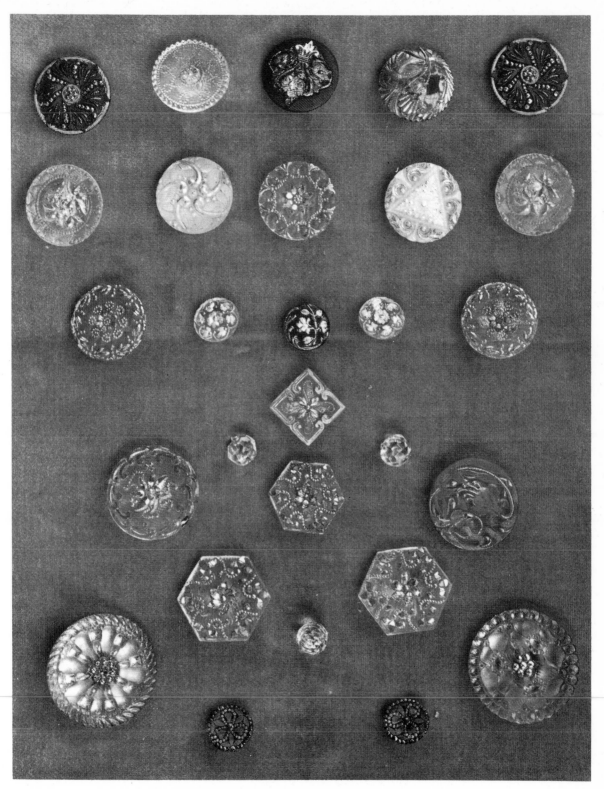

22 *Lacy glass and pressed glass*

glittering in the sun outside the houses, and of watching the workers heat, twist and work the glass. Small pieces of foil were inserted in the mould to produce the foil-inset buttons; others were made by twirling several rods together, or by using fine tubes to make bubbles.

Accurate information on British firms making glass buttons during the nineteenth century has proved hard to come by. Several firms questioned on the subject reported that it was likely that they had done so, but only James Grove & Sons were able to produce evidence. At the 1851 Exhibition, G. & William Twigg, Neal & Tonks, and Smith, Kemp & Wright, all of Birmingham, displayed them, no doubt partly with the export market in mind. Persons concerned with other aspects of the glass industry have told me that many of the firms engaged in glass-button production were small concerns with a short industrial life.

Of special note to collectors are the paperweight buttons, shown clearly in the centre and at the lower right-hand point of the star on plate 23. Collectors will probably readily identify the other examples shown. Paperweight is the name given to glass-ball buttons that are made after the manner of a nineteenth-century glass weight. Small pieces of glass, or cut canes, were mounted on a base and capped with a dome of clear glass; air bubbles could be trapped within it by the use of fine tubes, and sulphides made by using French chalk. Old paperweight buttons are scarce, but the craft has been revived in America during the past twenty years. Modern productions have been made primarily for the collector market, an idea which seems odd to the British way of thinking. The

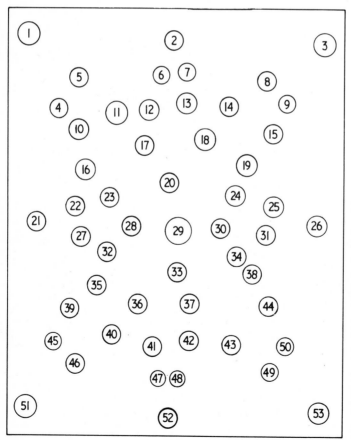

In plate 23, the buttons in the star are: Paperweights: 8, 11, 21, 26, 29, 42, 46, 53. Foil inset: 16, 18, 28, 34, 37, 41, 47. Imitation agates: 7, 9, 17. 'Bird's eggs': 13, 19, 38. Claw mounting: 50. Pin-head shank: 15. Faceted ball: 51. The other examples demonstrate typical patternings of the time.

Background—tissue over cooking foil!

23 *Glass-ball buttons*

making and marketing of them has been described at length in *Just Buttons* and other American publications. Such buttons are unlikely to be found in Britain, and judging from examples seen in America they are not of the same quality as the old buttons.

Imitation glass-ball buttons are currently produced in plastic materials. These are easily distinguished from the glass variety as they are much lighter in weight, less cold to the touch, and if tapped against the teeth do not resound.

Small Fancy Glass
CHARM-STRING BUTTONS

Making a 'charm string' was one of the many ways in which the young ladies of America used to amuse themselves between the schoolroom and marriage. During the 1880s and 1890s this made a suitable alternative to doing the flowers. When a newspaper proprietor offered a prize for the most attractive string, he was overwhelmed by the response. A charm string was a string of 1,000 small glass buttons, each different. The first one was known as the touch button, and the last was to be added by Prince Charming when he came to collect his bride! Those in between were added by the girl herself, and many were collected from friends and well-wishers. A complete string has seldom been found by a collector. Either Prince Charming anticipated events, the young lady gave up in despair, or—more likely—the string broke! Romantic stories persist.

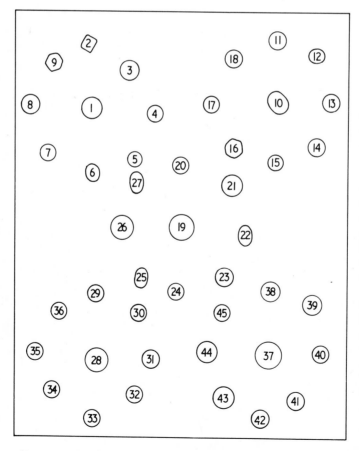

Paperweight types, solid and domed: 1, 10, 28; solid ball, 13; twisted canes (Jabonek), 29-36. Pin-head shanks: 23, 43. Outline design with birdcage metal shank: 8. Imitation hardstone: 9, 16, 25. Imitation cameo: 39. Foil inset: 38. Imitation sulphides: 6, 24. Amethyst in gold mount: 15. Czech (Jabonek) self-shank types: 7, 37, 40, 41, 44, 45. Matt-surface ball: 3. 4-way metal shanks: 4, 5. Cone tops (gaiter): 17, 18.

Background—brocade.

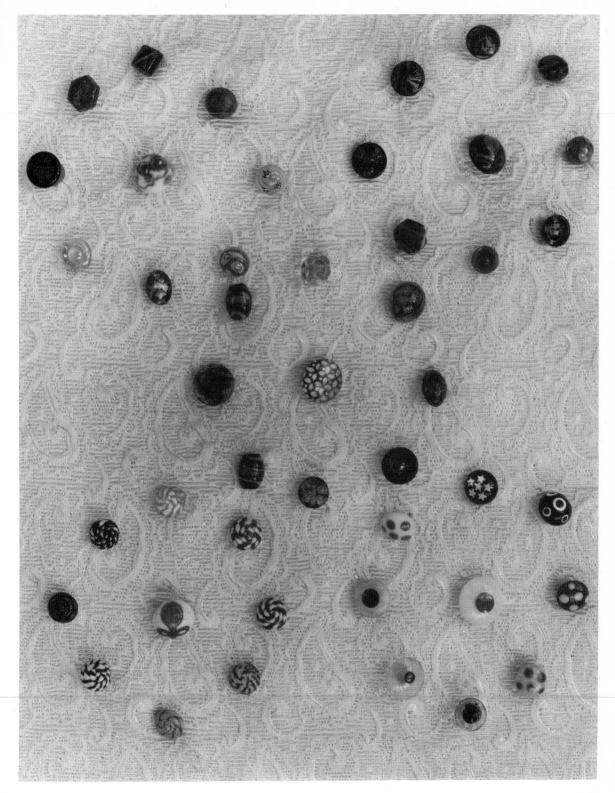

24 *Charm-string buttons*

Several writers at the beginning of the century speak of buttons being made in Britain from cane glass, with the use of plier-like tools to pinch and form them. Charm-string buttons are normally of the loop-shank type; it is rare to find a sew-through button included.

The buttons shown on plate 24 are the type used for charm strings, although some of them are of later date than the custom. They are mainly of European origin, with possibly some British products included.

FANCY WAISTCOAT BUTTONS

Many buttons of this type were produced during the latter half of the nineteenth century but their popularity reached its height during the Edwardian and post-Edwardian period. Production persisted throughout the 1920s, although by then quality and taste had deteriorated. An example of this is seen in nos 33, 35, 39-41, in plate 25. Such buttons are referred to as the 'Downfall of Man' series and are known on both sides of the Atlantic. A Connecticut tailor of long standing was asked about them recently and replied to the effect that although the firm had stocked them, nice men didn't buy them.

The buttons at the four corners of the plate, nos 1, 5, 55, 59, are from dress-shirt sets and have little collector interest because of their abundance. They are sometimes known as bachelor buttons as they are not sewn on but attached by means of eyelets.

Many waistcoat buttons were made with metal mounts, eg nos 6-14 and others. This not only improved their appearance but prevented the sharp edge of the glass from

Background—binca fabric.

60

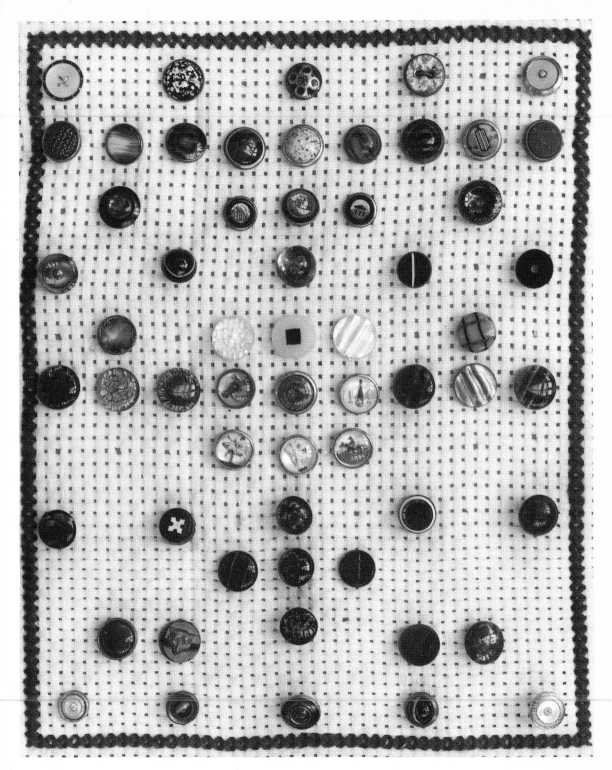

25 *Fancy waistcoat buttons*

chipping, or cutting the button-hole. Hardstone and imitation hardstone were popular materials; these are represented by nos 21 and 54 (genuine), and nos 7, 14, 23, 27, 45, 50 and 53 (imitations made from glass).

Nos 16-18 represent Italian glass mosaic work and are probably tourist items, while 43 is an example of a Victorian mourning button, in inlaid glass.

From a collector viewpoint, the most sought-after button is 34. This is known as a peacock eye, and can also be seen on the frontispiece (no 18). It is made by using green and blue foil under glass, in this case with a gilt mount. Such buttons are highly prized in the USA and are thought to have been made in Europe. The majority of the other buttons shown are made wholly or partly from glass, the interests of the sportsman being represented by 51 (metal escutcheon on black glass).

Among the many odd experiments carried out by Professor J. K. Galbraith (the pioneer of work study), was one to see whether it was quicker to button a waistcoat up or down: I understand he favoured starting at the bottom. He is also credited with estimating that prior to the general use of zip fasteners, an average man did up 11,200 buttons per year! While speaking of men's wear, it is worth noting that the earliest fly-buttons were not found on trousers. In 1783 the French Montgolfier brothers, inventors of the hot-air balloon, made a large balloon for a public demonstration, which took place at Annonay on 5 June. The balloon rose to 6,000 feet and landed ten minutes later a mile and a half away. It is reported that the different parts of the balloon were fastened together with buttons and buttonholes, and that the short duration of the flight was the result of gas loss through the buttonholes!

In 1794 a military observation balloon was used and the personnel accompanying it were known as the Aerostatic Corps of the French Artillery Service. They were supplied with blue uniforms complete with red-braid facings and buttons embossed with the word *Aerostier*. Buttons depicting balloons are fairly well known and liked by collectors.

Miscellaneous China and Glass

Inevitably there are buttons which either do not fit into distinct categories or cannot be obtained in sufficient quantities to fill a page. Some of these are shown on plate 26 (which has a linen background). Those in the top row are glass buttons, identical with some on old sample cards of James Grove & Sons. They are therefore assumed to be of this company's manufacture, c 1865-90.

The second and third rows show a selection of milk-glass buttons of British or European origin and dating from the end of the nineteenth century. Milk glass is so named because of its milky appearance, but is known in a variety of colours. The buttons on each end of the third row are fawn-coloured, and this is sometimes called caramel glass. The decoration on these buttons is known among collectors as outline design. A design has, in fact, been scratched on the surface and filled with gold paint. The Prince of Wales' feathers in the centre of the second row is an example of an escutcheon (qv) on glass and bears the motto *Ich Dien* (I serve).

The large button in the centre of the third row and the small one at the bottom right-hand corner are examples of hand-painted design on white milk glass. The other small buttons are examples of milk glass, lustre trim, iridescent finish and a hand-painted pansy.

In the centre, above the bottom line, is a Wedgwood jasper medallion (mounted against white fabric). This is not a button, but an example of the type of work used during the eighteenth and nineteenth centuries as a centrepiece for metal button shells.

62

26 *Various china and glass buttons*

Matthew Boulton of Birmingham was one of the people who made such mountings, many of which were decorated with cut steel or glass facets. The best-quality centre-pieces were made by Josiah Wedgwood, and the production of jasperware items (but not buttons) is continued to this day. Examples of Wedgwood jasperware buttons can be seen in the Victoria & Albert Museum in London, the Luckock Collection at Birmingham, and the Just Buttons Museum in Southington, Connecticut. During recent years imitations of these buttons, in type but not in quality, have been produced in the USA.

The bottom row of plate 26 shows an unusual selection of buttons. The first one on the left is a small white porcelain button with a self-shank and black-painted overglaze design. I have never seen another button like it, but from a study of antique china I suggest that this originated from Liverpool. Alternatively Coalport could be the source, as buttons marked by this firm (but of later date) are known in American collections.

The second button has the appearance of Staffordshire lustre-ware, but again there is no precise method of authentication. It is a typical pinkish colour. The centre button, and also one shown on the frontispiece, is an example of amateur painting on a ceramic blank. At the beginning of this century a popular pastime for the young ladies of England was the hand painting of china. Factories made white goods, mainly teasets, for this purpose. After decoration they were often returned to the makers for glazing and firing. These buttons, however, are painted with oils on the surface and are unglazed. The fourth button is deep brown glass with a birdcage metal shank and tickertape design. The fifth has already been dealt with.

Three buttons shown on the frontispiece are worth discussion at this point. Button 29 is an example of passementerie jet—the name being a complete misnomer. Passementerie is currently used in Italy to describe a variety of small trimmings, but in the eighteenth and nineteenth centuries was applied to buttons decorated with beads and fine braids. Jet used in this connection means imitation jet. A passementerie jet button is one made from imitation jet faced in the manner of steel or beads and cemented to a metal base. In this case the material used is black glass. Such buttons are very fragile, and in consequence good examples are uncommon.

Button 1 is an example of a Connecticut pottery button. Such buttons were made in Norwalk and Prospect in this state and are often called Norwalk buttons. There is mention of button making in this area as early as 1825, most being made before 1853. Recently, local collectors have excavated old sites and waded about in streams in the vicinity looking for both buttons and artefacts from the works.

Norwalk buttons are easily recognized by their mottled glazing and pin-head metal shanks. Due to a similarity in appearance with the glazed pottery produced in Bennington, Vermont, they have on occasions been called Vermont or Bennington buttons. This is incorrect. The nearest British equivalent to this glaze can be seen on Sussex slipware from the Rye pottery.

I regard Connecticut buttons as interesting examples of American antiques. Together with the charming New England furniture and decorated tinware produced in the area, they are of equal merit to anything made in Britain or Europe at the time. This is an

---

Plate 27 shows a selection of small glass buttons referred to earlier. None of them are jet, but all show the wide variety of pattern in which such buttons were produced during the 'plateau' period of button making.

Background—felts.

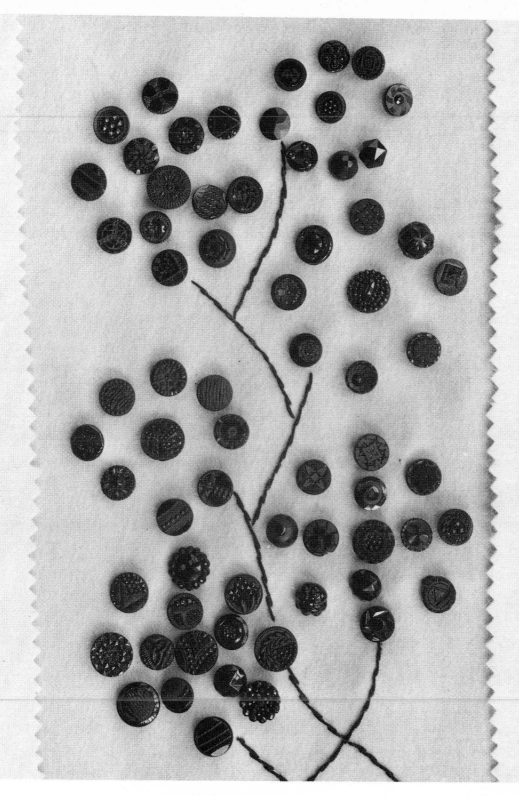

27 *Small black glass buttons*

aspect often overlooked by the antique-hungry American—perhaps just an instance of someone else's grass looking greener! The third button on the frontispiece to be mentioned here is no 13, a fine example of hand painting, probably on ivory under glass, and dated from the nineteenth century. Such buttons, of varying qualities, are known to collectors as underglass buttons.

Art Nouveau

From 1875 to 1900 public demand had switched from cloth-covered buttons to glass, but during the 1880s the decorative metal button for women's wear became fashionable. From the turn of the century metal took over from glass as the main material. New machinery and methods of making lighter, more attractive metal buttons, coupled with non-tarnishing finishes, enhanced their sales.

The rise of the Art Nouveau movement accelerated this trend. The form of decoration and design which we now call Art Nouveau developed during the 1890s and from 1900 to 1910 influenced all forms of manufactured goods. It began as a revolt movement. The artist tried first to fight against, and then to come to terms with, the mechanized results of the Industrial Revolution, for the switch from hand-made to machine-made goods had resulted in heavy, clumsy design. Victorian gothic furniture is an obvious example of this. Oscar Wilde and his associates represented the aesthetic side of the movement in Britain; craftsmen and artists were led by Sir Edward Burne-Jones, William Morris and their pre-Raphaelite colleagues. In America Louis C. Tiffany, Frank Carder and others were responsible for some of the finest specimens of Art Nouveau in the world.

During the past few years the interest in Art Nouveau has increased rapidly, with the result that when it is offered at auction in Sotheby's or Christie's the salerooms are crowded to capacity. The prices paid for good examples by known artists are little short of astronomical considering that ten years ago many were lying rejected in junk heaps.

Art Nouveau design is typified by flowing lines, the use of natural forms, leaves, flowers, women's hair and trailing draperies. Excellent examples can be found in unusual sitings. Street lamps, water fountains and railway fittings of the period often reflect the trend. At Helston in Cornwall there are some fine railings decorated with pine cones, and beautiful pottery tiles adorn a public convenience in Birmingham! Buttons were by no means overlooked, many of them being works of art in miniature. Designers utilized a wide variety of materials to convey the current sense of decoration. They also wished to prove to the public that it was possible for machine-made objects to reflect the beauties of nature.

British Hallmarked Silver

Britain has the longest and finest history of silverwork in the world and also the most carefully documented. The craft of the silversmith has been governed by Act of Parliament from the end of the twelfth century. Dates of articles can be traced from the end of the seventeenth century; records prior to 1666 were destroyed in the Great Fire of London. All silver articles weighing over half an ounce must, of course, be

---

The buttons shown on plate 28 are a representative sample of Art Nouveau design. Elsewhere in this book are equally typical productions categorized under their materials of manufacture.

Background—copy of an Art Nouveau photo-frame on paper.

28 *Art Nouveau buttons*

assayed, ie tested for quality, and stamped if satisfactory; the maker's mark, the date letter, the town of assay office mark and other marks may be shown. The study of hall-marks is outside the scope of this book, but it should be noted that the lion passant indicates British sterling silver.

Silver buttons as decorative items were produced during the years 1900 to 1910 when they were fashionable for women's jackets and blouses. They had, of course, been made for uniforms, regalia and Scottish evening dress over a long period. The design of the women's buttons was greatly influenced by the Art Nouveau movement, silver being an ideal medium for such design.

Plate 29 shows some hallmarked silver buttons, as follows : 1, R & W, Birmingham, 1902; 2, T.W., London, 1901; 3, J.G., Birmingham, 1902; 4, S., London, 1900; 5, ? W.H., Birmingham, 1901; 6, L & S, Birmingham, 1903; 7, L & S, Birmingham, 1901; 8, S.J., London, 1904; 9, M.Bro., Birmingham, 1901; 10, W.H.H., Birmingham, 1907; 11, H.M., Birmingham, 1902; 12, S & P, Birmingham, 1900; 13, Cymbric L & - (Liberty's), Birmingham, 1901; 14, T.W., London, 1900; 15, C.H., Chester, 1895.

Button 3 is a Joseph Gloster production. This design is known to Americans as Music, and has been seen on other items.

Button 10 is a Haseler & Restall production.

Background—felt.

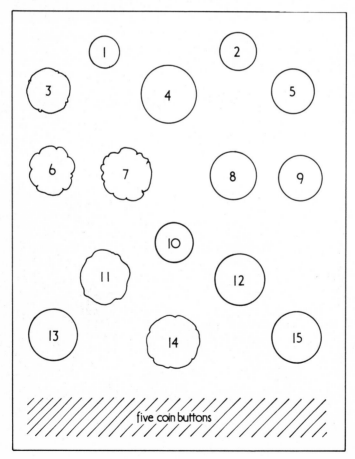

five coin buttons

29 *Silver buttons and coin buttons*

The majority of silver buttons were assayed in Birmingham, a few in London, and an occasional example with the Chester mark is found. As the names of Birmingham makers were not published after 1850, the Assay Master at Birmingham has kindly identified many of a selected list of marks from buttons, though the firms concerned apparently ceased to trade during the 1920s, apart from two which are still active. Messrs Joseph Gloster (who used the mark J.G.) state that 'Silver buttons were in fact, only a sideline for us. They were made during the period 1900-5 and were sold in sets on cards. We do not have any details of patterns or samples left in stock.' This firm of manufacturing silversmiths was established in 1880.

The other firm, Messrs Haseler & Restall (W.H.H.), report that 'The only information we can give is the fact that buttons were a sideline to the Masonic jewellery and pewterware business, and they have always been made, as far as we can tell, since the early part of this century. We do still produce silver buttons, but they are not for general sale, as they are designed and manufactured to customers' individual specification, and cannot be sold without their permission.' This firm, manufacturing jewellers, silversmiths, pewtersmiths and medallists, was established in 1851 and specializes in civic and Masonic jewellery.

It is interesting to be able to establish a definite link with the silver buttons of the past, but a pity that more information is not available. It seems that their production was a short-lived gimmick.

Coin Buttons

The conversion of coins to buttons has been practised for many years, despite the fact that in Britain and most other countries it is illegal to deface any coin in current circulation.

Eighteenth-century British and European coins are those most frequently seen as buttons. Oriental coins were sometimes used, and at the end of the nineteenth century American coin buttons were made, but are seldom seen outside America. Waistcoat buttons made from small American silver coins were given to boys for their twenty-first birthday, and became known as Freedom buttons. Many of these were semi-amateur productions, but from 1910 to 1915 the C.M.R. Manufacturing Co made them commercially. Production was discontinued as a result of government action around 1917, therefore the buttons are now very scarce.

The age of a coin button is not necessarily the same as that of the coin from which it is made, the date of the coin being only the first possible date. Coin buttons are relatively scarce, but apparently of only limited collector interest. Enamelled coins are occasionally seen as buttons, cufflinks or brooches.

Buttons made as imitations of coins have always been popular. There is no restriction on their manufacture as they have blank backs and are made of gilded brass to represent gold, or white metal to imitate silver. The Austrians and Dutch have produced many

---

On plate 30 all the buttons except those with the fish design are two-piece metals, brass, bronzed or spelter. Some have specific names among American collectors, but these have been 'coined' and do not necessarily coincide with manufacturers' designs; for example, the children fishing (R.H.S.) is known as a Kate Greenaway. The large button near the top, centre, is a peacock (not a pineapple); and the cherub design at the bottom centre shows the use of metal gauze in button design. All these buttons were obtained in Great Britain or the Republic of Ireland, and are unmarked.

Background—Edwardian coat-lining fabric.

such buttons, and Spanish replicas of pieces of eight are currently on sale in Alicante. Imitation-coin buttons are sometimes known as Forbidden Money amongst American collectors.

Metal Picture Buttons

This is a collector name for metal buttons like those on plate 30, which depict some object or scene, as opposed to a geometrical pattern. Their production commenced during the latter part of the nineteenth century, reached its height between 1885 and 1905 and gradually fell away later. Precise dating is almost an impossibility. Most manufacturers repeated their designs continuously, designs were copied, re-issued and even pirated from one firm to another. The majority were made for the department-store market.

Some idea of date can be gained from studying contemporary fashion trends. For example, Kate Greenaway designs were used on buttons during the 1890s following the successful publication of children's books with Greenaway illustrations. Actresses and theatrical subjects came and went in conjunction with public taste, but were considered vulgar by *ladies* in Britain.

Very few picture buttons are backmarked, as the makers' names were printed on the cards on which they were mounted. Many are of very inferior quality. As a general guide, the best came from France, the next best from Britain, and the cheap items originated in Germany and Austria. Very few American productions are found in Britain but picture buttons were in fact more plentiful in America than in Europe. American collectors subdivide their picture buttons into numerous categories, and those interested should study the current American publications.

Flowers

British people in particular have a great love of flowers. Much leisure time is spent on cultivating them, and arranging them to decorate both homes and public buildings. (Indeed, in his book *Prison Governor*, Major B. D. Grew mentions that one of the privileges permitted to star convicts in British prisons is to have flowers in their cells!)

In our grandmothers' day, flowers were considered very suitable for ladies' wear of all types as, unlike some other subjects, they were not only quite without offence, but conveyed meanings. We have all heard of the pansy for thoughts, the lily for purity and the obvious message of the forget-me-not. Other flowers also had special significance, and books could be purchased containing explanations. The young ladies of the day regarded flowers as many modern girls regard horoscopes in women's magazines. It is therefore not surprising to find that flowers are frequently depicted on buttons, and indeed this habit is in no way confined to Britain.

The buttons shown on plate 31 illustrate a small selection from those available at the turn of the century (the background here is embroidery on cotton fabric). They also illustrate what are referred to by collectors as escutcheons. These are stamped-out metal ornamentations fixed by prongs to a backing, often with a piece of some other material between the two. In the case of the rose button (fifth down on the right) the material is celluloid. The grape design on the left and the hellebore, lower left, are examples of escutcheons without the intermediate material. The acorn (lower right) is not an escutcheon as it is pressed out in one piece with the front and rim.

Escutcheons are frequently found in conjunction with mother-of-pearl and wood backs. When the decoration is held in place by some retaining material over the top, for example glass, collectors refer to it as embedded decoration.

31 *Flower and plant designs*

Flowers are popular subjects for studio buttons. Studio buttons are those which have been made in America during the past twenty-five years, primarily for the collector market. Considering the seriousness with which the average American takes his hobby, it is not surprising that many enterprising people, retired business men and others, have set up making buttons to sell to collectors. One finds Tunbridge buttons that never saw Kent, 'paperweights' that never saw Bohemia, and eighteenth-century reproductions by the dozen. What is perhaps strange, until one understands the situation, is that collectors buy such buttons, many of them being of only very average quality. But until recently few American collectors could visit Britain or Europe to buy for themselves, and when they did so they found antique dealers and others completely ignorant about buttons, unaware of their collector interest. The American is ingenious and also very conscious of his country's 'youth'; to make buttons is one way in which he can combine his ingenuity and skill to produce what people want—'old' buttons! Collectors buy them, and regard them as limited editions, so everyone is happy.

It is highly unlikely that such buttons will find their way to Britain, so potential British collectors are not in danger of being sold reproductions as the real thing. A study of old methods and materials should quickly enable anyone to distinguish studio buttons from originals.

Filigree and Stamped Metal Buttons

Filigree is a term which has been misused for some time. In 1900 contemporary writers referred to the habit of erroneously calling perforated metal-ball buttons filigree; however both the habit and the condemnation of it have persisted. Filigree work proper is the soldering together of metal wires, originally gold or silver, to form a delicate spider-web-type pattern. Such work when applied to buttons was often spherical, but was also used during the eighteenth century to make disc-shaped buttons.

None of the buttons shown on plate 32 are true filigree work; true filigree work is like *pliqué-à-jour* (qv) without the enamel filling. The six on the right-hand side are the nearest equivalent, and show the type of pattern that could be produced. These buttons are made from nineteenth-century watch-cocks, and are cut out by hand, as opposed to being soldered. A watch-cock was the protective plate placed over the balance wheel of a chain-driven watch. It was normally made in brass and the degree of fine ornamentation was an indication of the skill and artistic ability of the watchmaker. The basic shape was cut out, and then engraved with the design. The holes were then drilled and filed out. The cocks shown here have been silver plated, probably after they were made into buttons. The top of the cock has been sawn off.

The other buttons on plate 32 are examples of filigree-type stamped metal, and include several with steel facet trimmings. They all date from 1880 to 1930 but several show a decided Art Nouveau influence in the design.

The background to the buttons on plate 32 is felt.

Brilliants

In the eighteenth century Frenchmen made buttons decorated with diamonds, then came marcasite followed by cut steel, and lastly lustre-glass and brilliants.

Collector and manufacturer names for the buttons shown on plate 33 vary: glass brilliants, rhinestone, jewels, paste and glitter are all used. American collectors refer to a button as a jewel when it has one large decorative stone or glass piece in the centre, and call it jewelled when it is trimmed with numerous pieces.

The quality of such buttons can be determined by the setting. As with items of

74

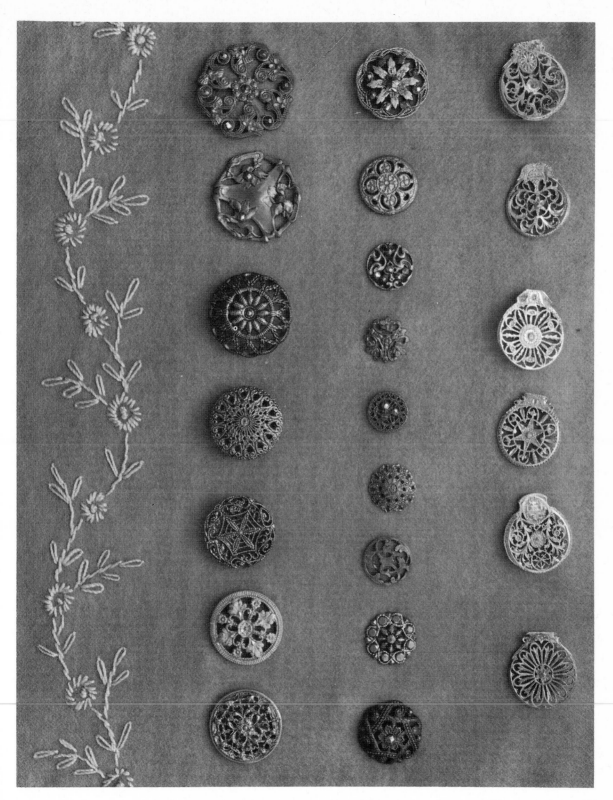

32 *Filigree and stamped metal buttons*

costume jewellery, manufacturers do not spend time and money making elaborate settings for cheap products. Buttons like the large one in the centre of the plate are made by pressing out white-metal mounts and cementing the glass chips in position. Plastic settings are also used, as in the buttons on each side of the centre one.

The superior buttons are those where the brilliants have been secured in position with claw settings, or are held by the rim of individually placed mounts. The majority of these were made in France and Czechoslovakia. Their popularity at the beginning of the century for evening wear resulted in millions being imported. Dress trimmings were also made by similar methods, and these are often thought to be buttons by the undiscerning. Such trimmings have one or more holes for attachment at the sides. Buttons have shanks at the back, or holes from front to back.

I remember as a child becoming very excited over an American dress I was given that was trimmed with glittery buttons. They were retained for years, and transferred to other less suitable garments. Modern brilliant buttons are plentiful, but the better examples are not cheap. The demand for them is chiefly as dress accessories, collectors being only interested in limited quantities of authenticated old ones.

Plate 33 also shows examples of buttons known as mirror backs. These are glass buttons which are silvered at the back like a mirror, and have coloured glass facets or a design etched on the front. The thistle button (on the right of the fifth row) is an example of the latter type. Similar buttons with a transfer design at the back are known as kaleidoscopes among collectors.

W. C. Aitkin, in *British Manufacturing Industries* (1876), described the manufacture of such buttons as follows:

> Other varieties of glass buttons are cut out of coloured sheet glass the back of which has been quickened or coated on one side with rolled tin amalgamated with quicksilver, to render it reflective. The neck of the button is soldered to a small disk of metal, which is afterwards tinned on the opposite surface to that to which the shank is fastened, so that when the latter is heated, the solder fuses, melts the quick and the adhesion of the neck to the button is complete. These glass buttons are finished by grinding the edge and surface, if cut and fawcetted. When flashed [two-colour] glass is used the ornament is cut through the flashed colour with revolving copper tools like a cameo.

Mr Aitkin's report seems to indicate that such buttons were made in the Birmingham district, but to date I have not found any firms which produced them. Many small businesses closed between the two world wars, others have amalgamated since, and as the buttons are fragile, examples are infrequently found.

On plate 33, the top row shows two pressed-brass buttons with steel facet and brilliant trim, and two brilliant ball buttons with loop shanks. In row 2 are four imitation pearl and brilliant buttons, and in the centre a good-quality brilliant button, probably French. Row 3 shows brilliants on plastic; a purple/clear mirror back; a modern square button; and a kaleidoscope, red/yellow/green, in a claw setting. Row 4 shows a small French button; a dress shirt 'drum'; a quality French button, in centre; and two modern types with self-shanks. Row 5 has a 'ruby' and 'diamond' design; an Austrian-tiny type with fabric inset; a modern glass-lustre/brilliant; a thistle-design mirror back. In Row 6 are a Paris back with crackle centre; three examples of modern mountings; a square brilliant with claw settings. Row 7 has four small claw-mounted domes. Row 8, brilliants in brass mounts; claw-set brilliants with smoked centre; and a modern pressed mounting. Row 9 shows brilliants and celluloid inset with iridescent trim; and two modern copies of French buttons.

Background—black lace over grosgrain.

33 *Brilliants, 'jewels', paste and glitter*

Austrian Tinies

This name is one of the few collector terms which appear to have originated in Britain. It is perhaps not so widely known as some, but is the most suitable I have heard for describing the little buttons shown on plate 34.

These were much in vogue from 1890 to 1920, and serve to bridge the gap between what I have called the plateau and the descent in the history of button manufacture. Very little appears to be known about them, other than that they were made by the million! Museums to which they have been shown can offer no assistance, and American collectors expressed interest but had no knowledge about them. They are found in every button-box of the period, and in most old country-store sales.

The cards on which Austrian tinies are found carry twenty-four buttons, and prices on the back indicate that 5d or 6d ($2\frac{1}{2}$p; 6 cents) was charged per card. They are generally labelled 'Best Austrian Make' or 'Made in Austria' and a note is sometimes added to the effect that each half-dozen is fastened separately, or that only best materials were used in manufacture. Americans do not refer to six as half a dozen so perhaps the buttons were not sold in the States.

Austria has been a source of button manufacture for the last hundred years, and buttons today can be purchased in wide variety there. Each village has at least one shop selling trimmings and buttons. The variety of the buttons and their good quality make them a very inexpensive purchase for the visitor from Britain or America. A survey of world button makers taken in 1880 showed that there were thirty-seven in Vienna alone. Exportation of vegetable-ivory buttons to Italy formed a large part of the market, until Mussolini forbade it and forced the Italians to make their own.

Austrian tinies are all small two-piece metal buttons with a loop shank and usually a black back. The trimming on the front demonstrates an incredible variety of design. Considering the price for which they were sold, the workmanship is little short of fantastic, even allowing for mechanization. Each button design in its numerous separate parts must have been tooled up by someone, a precision engineering feat in itself.

Plate 34 shows a variety of trimmings including celluloid insets, pearl shell, velvet, woven fabrics and ribbon, and coloured metals. A collection of such buttons could form a subject of study by itself, and as they are obtainable in such profusion it should not prove expensive.

Background—card.

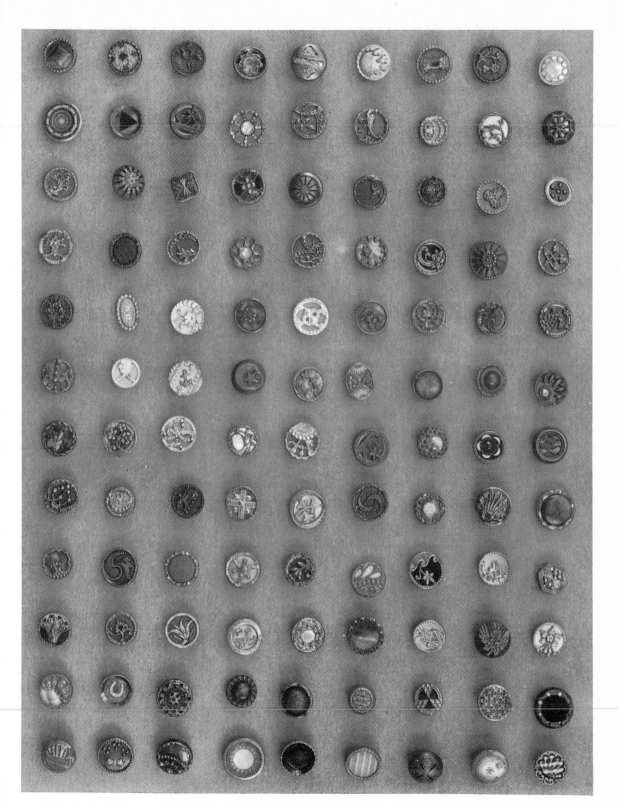

34 *Austrian tinies*

THREE:
THE DESCENT 1911-1940

Lithographs and Patriotism

One dictionary definition of a lithograph is: 'Print taken from stone block, which after design is traced on with greasy chalk, is so treated with acid, gum and water that the unchalked parts reject ink and make no impression.' This process was invented by Alois Senefelder, a Bavarian, in 1795. It was first used in France in 1816, in London in 1822 and in the United States by William and John Pendleton of Boston in 1824. It was popularized in America by the Currier & Ives Company. Nathaniel Currier was an apprentice at the Pendleton Co before commencing business on his own account, where he was later joined by his brother Charles and by James Merritt Ives, a brother-in-law of Charles. This company was responsible for numerous lithographs of popular appeal, details from some of which were used as button designs.

To a button collector the term lithograph includes photographs and other methods of printing, and is used to describe a variety of buttons which were first made during the 1880s but which did not become very fashionable until the early years of George V (1911). During that time there was a fashion craze, first for buttons which portrayed actresses and other personalities and later, when waistcoats became popular with men's sportswear, sets of buttons depicting any pretty girl or sporting activity were worn. Such buttons were popularized by the development of celluloid (qv) but in Britain were considered common by the upper classes. Ladies of breeding would not 'know' a man who wore theatrical buttons, in the same way as my grandmother did not 'know' any woman who dyed her hair.

The prints or photographs were mounted in metal settings and a piece of clear celluloid was placed over the top as protection. During the years the celluloid tends to discolour and the photographs fade, so the end result is dingy-looking. There is a limited market for lithograph buttons in America, but in Britain they are seldom worth anything like as much as would-be vendors imagine.

The buttons on the left of plate 35 are a small selection of 'lithographs'. The majority are made from photographs or coloured prints, but indicate the type of button produced. The sporting subjects are marked with the crossed-sword trade mark of Buttons Ltd, and the legend 'British Made'.

THE QUEEN—GOD BLESS HER

The wearing of buttons and pins to signify one's patriotism or support for political figures has declined sharply in Britain during recent decades, and was never as popular a custom with the British as it was, and still is, with the Americans, who enjoy wearing buttons and badges to signify loyalty. Collectors refer to the celluloid-covered badge as a pin-back. Opinion is divided as to whether such items should be included in a collection of more orthodox buttons.

At the time of the inauguration of George Washington special buttons were produced

35 *'Lithographs' and patriotic buttons* 81

for delegates to wear on their coats and breeches. These were made of copper, brass or Sheffield plate and were fine pieces of workmanship. There were a variety of designs incorporating loyal slogans, the American eagle and the initials of the thirteen States of the Union. Today they are highly prized by collectors, who call them inaugurals and treat them with the same respect as the national flag. (Americans respect their flag, as the British respect the Queen. It is their permanent emblem of national pride.)

Since the time of Washington, the arrivals and departures of presidents, the rise and fall of statesmen, and the addition of new States to the Union have been faithfully reflected in an enormous quantity of buttons. Some of the early ones are now being reproduced. The majority of modern pin-backs are celluloid or plastic and they range from quaint to vulgar. British people will remember the 'I like Ike' campaign after World War II. More recent slogans are not always as complimentary.

Two books dealing with this type of button are *Political Campaign Buttons in Color* by Otha Wearin and *Ballots and Bandwaggons* by Ralph Martin. While I understand they are basically colour-picture books on pin-back buttons, they also provide an interesting glimpse into American social history.

Prior to 1940 British people apparently did not commemorate political events by producing buttons, but coronations and jubilees have always caught the imagination of the manufacturers. *The Complete Button Book,* published in America in 1949, and illustrating thousands of buttons, shows a set of silver buttons which seem to have been made for the Silver Jubilee of George III in 1809. The authors comment 'that the British people celebrate the long reigns of their sovereigns in every conceivable way'! These are obviously a rarity, but buttons issued in connection with the long reign of Queen Victoria are more easily found. The 1887 and 1897 jubilees were certainly the cause of much celebration throughout an empire on which the sun never set—what a pity that the empire and most of the buttons have now gone the same way! The three small buttons at the top right of plate 35 are made from brass and embossed like a seal; this may in fact have been their original purpose, as the shanks are not very neatly attached. The woven ribbon down the centre was made in the city of Coventry, as are the two small Union Jack buttons made for the coronation of King George VI in 1937. The other portrait buttons are pin-backs representing the 1897 jubilee of Victoria and subsequent coronations. The jubilee button has an interesting back-mark which reads: 'The Whitehead & Hoag Co. 113 Leadenhall St. London England. Made in the U.S.A. Pat. July 21 1896'. This button was a missionary indeed!

The striped buttons at the bottom of the plate were made for children's wear and produced at the time of coronation and victory celebrations. Buttons of this kind are plentiful in Britain, America and France, and as all three countries have the same national colours it is impossible to distinguish between them.

The buttons on plate 35 are on a card background.

Celluloid

During the nineteenth century an American billiard-ball manufacturer offered a prize of $1,000 (£420) to any person who could produce a suitable synthetic substitute for ivory, and this offer sparked off all manner of inventions, celluloid being one. The actual

---

Plate 36 shows a selection of buttons incorporating celluloid, probably made at the beginning of this century.
Background—Edwardian lining fabric.

36 *Buttons incorporating celluloid*

invention of celluloid, the earliest form of plastic, is attributed to John Wesley Hyatt of New Jersey, and his brother. British experiments at about the same time were made by Messrs A. Parks and D. Spill. The term celluloid was originally the trade name of one company, but like the name 'hoover' has now become generic.

The main disadvantage of celluloid is its inflammability, and it was for this reason that buttons, toys and other items quickly lost popularity to other more fire-proof substances that were developed in its stead. Manufacturers were frightened off by the astronomical insurance premiums required when working with celluloid, but not before a few hundred million buttons had been produced. Collectors are warned against allowing any type of celluloid button to come in contact with fire, matches or liquid fuel; they are also best kept away from small children.

Ivoroid was originally a trade name for a celluloid material produced by a Connecticut firm called Landers, Frary & Clark, but it is now used by American collectors to describe any button with a celluloid covering that has been grained and embossed to represent ivory. One of the purposes of making ivoroid buttons was to overcome a difficulty in using vegetable ivory: corozo nuts are normally too small to allow buttons larger than one inch in diameter to be made. Ivoroid buttons could be any size, but tiny ones are unusual. They were made in greatest quantity during the early 1900s and those with picture or portrait designs are prized by American collectors. They are scarce in Britain.

The earlier and better varieties of celluloid and ivoroid button were made in imitation of better buttons, and although they represent the beginning of the synthetic age, when in good condition they are well worth collecting. Plate 36 shows a selection of these with their characteristic trimmings of glass brilliants, brass, stamped metal and, in one case, celluloid imitating goldstone. These buttons were probably of continental origin. During the 1920s and 1930s celluloid buttons were made by covering a wood mould with a thin sheet of celluloid, perhaps with foil or a stencil design showing through. Many of them are attractive when seen away from other buttons, and they all represent the Charleston and tea-dance era. At the latter end of the thirties floppy coats fastened with enormous buttons were in fashion, and the large buttons in plate 37 made from hard plastic material illustrate this craze.

Twentieth-Century Glass and Pottery

The 1920s and 1930s produced some extraordinary clothes, and these were often decorated with large glass and pottery buttons. This era is now described as Art Deco. The current revival of the thirties' styles has done little to improve the image of that era —no longer can distance lend enchantment to the view.

Manufacturers and others had recovered from 'the war to end all wars', and in the brief period before they recommenced making ammunition and army buttons, devoted themselves to fashion, then gay, chunky and vulgar. Sunbathing, a new pastime, produced its own fantastic garments, as did cocktail parties, where 'ripping-looking' girls with Eton crops and long cigarette holders did their best to dazzle the well-oiled male. Some of the best illustrations of the era are found in the earlier editions of the *William* books by Richmal Crompton.

The American influence was strong (no doubt helped along by the Prince of Wales)

Plate 37 shows a selection of celluloid and other plastic buttons dating from the 1930s.
  Background—Tana lawn, the design—by Liberty's of London—being a revival of the 1930s.

37 *Celluloid and other plastic buttons of the 1930s*

and this is clearly reflected in buttons of the time. Czechoslovakian glass was cheap and plentiful, new plastic materials were being developed, and bright synthetic dyes were replacing the more traditional colourings.

In plate 38, in the centre of the top row, is a red clay button with deep-blue glaze, marked 'CHB'. This is the signature of Charles H. Brannam of C. H. Brannam, Barnstaple, N. Devon. Correspondence with the company has produced the information that a small number of buttons were made there prior to 1939. The dark-blue colouring now characteristic of the company's wares was developed in the early 1900s. The pottery opened in 1879, and at the beginning of this century produced the now much-collected Barum ware. It is still in business. This button, the only example I have seen, was given to me by an Ilfracombe antique dealer.

The two buttons on either side of the Brannam button are also made of pottery and although these examples are unmarked, others have been seen marked Ruskin. Ruskin pottery was made at Smethwick between 1898 and 1935, when the company closed. The owner, Mr Howson Taylor, died in that year.

In the third row, the pressed milk-glass animal buttons are from children's wear of the 1930s and 40s. The teddy bear is from a coat made for me by my mother when I was a small child, and subsequently preserved in the family button-box. It has now lost its paint, but not my affection.

The four large glass buttons with lustre trim, shown below the animals, are English Glass Company productions. They were not made until the 1940s but represent an interesting story.

During the past few years my activities with buttons have produced much correspondence. A high percentage of people who have written to me trying to sell either factory stock or know-how have been European exiles or refugees who came to this country at the beginning of World War II. Many of them had little to offer but the knowledge of button-making when they arrived; some have subsequently become very successful in this or other fields. I visited the English Glass Company in Leicester during 1970, and while there I discovered from the company's history that their one-time glass-button production had resulted from the immigration of Joseph and Norma Oplatek in 1939. Mrs Oplatek had studied at Gablonz Art School and both she and her husband came from a long line of Bohemian glass workers, who had established themselves in the Iser mountains during the eighteenth century. The English Glass Company had previously made bicycle reflectors, but during the period of Mr and Mrs Oplatek's direction produced glass buttons, hatpins, beads and teddy-bear eyes, among other things. It is now concerned with optical components and similar items. The buttons shown here were lent by Mr T. J. Lawson, the present managing director of the company.

Painted Metal

The process of imitation continued. As time went by, manufacturers continued to find cheaper methods of mass-producing items to look 'like what they ain't'. The diamond button of the eighteenth century finally finished up as glass-trimmed celluloid, and the Battersea and Limoges enamels met an inglorious end as painted metal.

The other items on plate 38 are glass buttons from the 1930s, mainly of Czechoslovakian origin. The bottom row has some good examples of iridescent glass finish, which is produced by a fuming process.

Background—honeycomb smocking on Swiss cotton, by Liberty's of London.

86

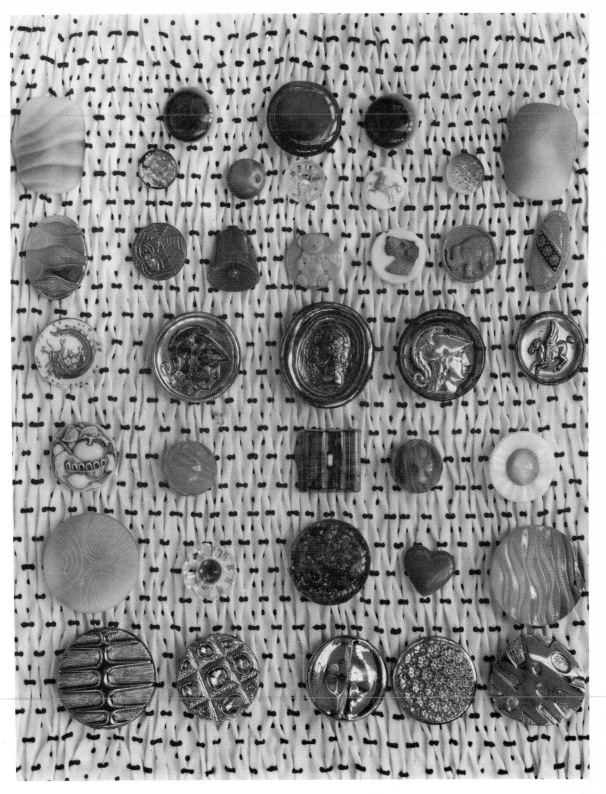

38 *Twentieth-century glass and pottery buttons*

By the 1920s and 1930s the button industry was feeling the effects of trade unionism, and in any case the slump and depression of Wall Street rippled across the world. People lost their jobs, and in America some of them no doubt turned to button collecting to pass the time. At the end of World War I raw materials were rationed and distribution was in the hands of rationing officers. Apparently these men were not very concerned with the needs of the button industry. A group of aggrieved manufacturers in Birmingham got together and formed the British Button Manufacturers' Association from an amalgamation of various interested groups. James Grove & Sons, Buttons Ltd, Firmin & Sons, together with nine other long-established firms, were founder members. (The Association is still going strong and produces a magazine and organizes dinners and functions as does any other 'bosses' society'.)

The distribution of materials was not the only problem with which the new association had to contend. In 1919 they were faced with what they considered to be a revolutionary demand from their workers for a forty-seven hour week. The workers won and the shorter week came into effect from March 1920. But when the working day went down, judging by the products, so did the quality.

Painted metal buttons were mass-produced during the twenties and thirties and some types are still in production. They were made to imitate enamels (qv), but their tendency to rust made them unpopular. When new they often look very attractive, and at a casual glance the better ones could be mistaken for enamels. However they quickly rust and flake in wear, and some dry-cleaning processes remove the paint.

Many of the examples shown in plate 39 were purchased in bulk from drapers' stores etc. Some of the more attractive ones came from a husband-and-wife business in Lancashire. The lady had sorted them out as a result of a bet. Her husband had maintained that no one would want them, and was, I imagine, even more surprised than she was by the price offered. Most painted metal buttons were mass-produced in Europe, but plenty of British firms, including Buttons Ltd, made them. Japan is also a possible source, particularly for examples found in America.

Plastic

The vast majority of modern civilian buttons are now made from one or another of the wide range of plastic materials which have been developed since World War I. Quality and production methods have been improved by modern machinery, but the finished button of 1970 is not very different from the button of 1935. It is the wearing and washing properties that have improved.

The buttons shown on plate 40 represent plastic from the mid-1920s onwards. Those in the top row were made during 1970 and distributed by a dyeing and finishing specialist in Glasgow. This firm, William & A. M. Robb, kindly supplied both buttons and information.

CASEIN

This material was discovered in 1903, but did not become a commercial proposition until the 1920s. A by-product of milk, like all other plastics it is an organic material which at some stage of its history is capable of flow. Under the action of heat and pressure it will take up any desired shape, and this is retained subsequently.

The majority of the painted metals on plate 39 are old shop stock and unused. Background—knitted rayon fabric, c 1940.

39 *Painted metals*

Casein buttons are of three types. They can be cut from sheets of plain cream casein and subsequently dyed any self colour. Highspot buttons are cut from rods of a material of this name (in the same way as wheels for toys can be sliced from a broom pole). The third type of casein material is mottled; it also is made up in sheet form, but from layers laid alternately one on top of the other. These can take up to eight weeks to formalize.

PERLOID
Buttons made from this material can be either turned or pressed out, but are only suitable for cheap garments which will not have to be frequently washed or cleaned, eg plastic macintoshes.

ACRYLIC AND POLYESTER
Buttons from these materials can be made by either turning or pressing and are more suitable for washing and dry cleaning.

The dyeing of the button blanks is now normally done by what is known as surface- or ring-dyeing methods, as opposed to colouring the material before button making. The second button in the top row on plate 40 has been scratched to show the surface dyeing. Buttons can also be made from laminated sheets of plastic material in the same way as liquorice sweets! This was a popular method during the 1930s and examples are shown.

On plate 40, the buttons shown in the two top rows, from left, are : highspot casein— turned; milled acrylic—scratched to show dyeing method; pressed acrylic; turned acrylic; turned perloid; turned polyester; milled casein (two examples); turned casein; and milled silk-mottled casein. The other buttons are varieties of plastic dating from 1930 to 1970.

Background—section from advertisement sheet.

40 *Plastic buttons from mid-1920s on*

FOUR:
SPECIALISED CATEGORIES 1800-1940

Enamels

During the eighteenth, nineteenth and early part of the twentieth centuries enamel buttons were made by the hundred thousand; the majority were French productions, often being back-marked as such, but a few made in Britain at the time of the 1851 Exhibition and thereafter.

British people tend to overrate enamels, perhaps because of their 'pretty' appearance, or because so many small boxes of these buttons were brought back from France by pre-war tourists, shut away in drawers, and only rediscovered fifty years later when Granny or Aunt Amy died. There are many valuable enamel buttons, but these boxed sets are usually mass-produced items.

It is a great pity more of them are not in general wear. I have several sets which I use on blouses and they are always admired. Enamel buttons have, of course, to be removed before laundering, but as they normally have loop shanks and clips to fit, they can be quickly removed from any garment with eyelets—and these are easily made by the home dressmaker.

The process of enamelling dates back almost to the beginning of civilization, having been discovered independently by the ancient Middle Eastern cultures, the Chinese and the Anglo-Saxons. Basically, enamelling is the application of powdered glass to prepared metal and the fusing of the two together with heat.

During the eighteenth century the French excelled themselves at enamelling and produced superb examples of enamelled buttons, often trimmed with gemstones, paste, gold or silver. Some of these can be seen at the Just Buttons Museum in Southington, Connecticut, and there are many in leading American collections. In 1970 a number of excellent examples fetched high prices at a sale held by Parke-Bernet (Sotheby's) in New York.

In Britain there is a collection of buttons assembled by the Rothschild family and now housed at Waddesdon Manor, a National Trust property in Buckinghamshire. This includes fine enamel buttons. Other examples of this type of button are on view in the Luckock collection in Birmingham, and on costume in the Victoria & Albert Museum in London.

METHODS OF ENAMELLING

There are various methods of enamelling and most of them have been used in button production. Some are rare. The majority of enamelled buttons encountered by the average collector will have been made after 1850.

Plate 41 shows a selection of enamel buttons, the majority being French.
Background—card.

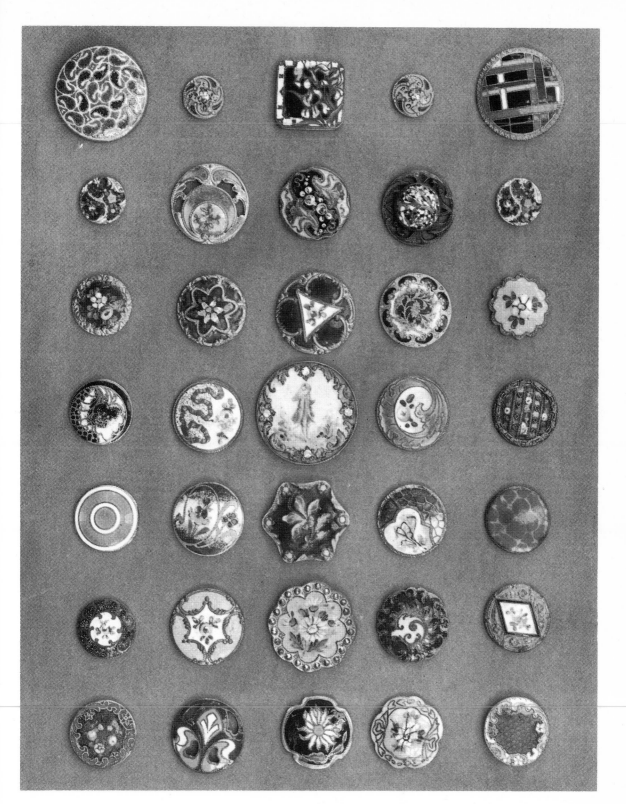

41   *Enamel buttons*

Basse taille. This process was developed by the Italians during the thirteenth century and in the last hundred years has been used for the manufacture of small quantities of buttons. It is more frequently seen on box lids, ash trays etc. *Basse taille* is the name given to the application of a coat of transparent enamel to a pre-prepared engine-turned design, which is visible on the finished article. Sometimes the design is stamped out in foil and placed over the base metal, but for better quality the base metal is turned. *Basse taille* is sometimes used in conjunction with other types of enamelling. Plate 41 shows examples of *basse taille* work in the bull's eye striped button at the left and the fish-scale design at the bottom right-hand corner.

Champlevé. By this method the base metal is carved or stamped with a design in much the same way as a coin. The small 'wells' left in the pattern are then filled with coloured enamels, and fired. The process may need to be repeated several times owing to contraction, and the finished article is then polished. At the beginning of this century there was a fashion for enamelling coins by this method.

Champlevé buttons are fairly easy to acquire, the majority having been made in France and Germany. The recent craze for home enamelling kits in Britain has resulted in some rather curious examples of this and other enamelled work being produced. Such items, and those seen in seaside craft shops, are examples of peasant art of the seventies and have no intrinsic value.

The centre button in the bottom row of plate 41 illustrate *champlevé* clearly.

Cloisonné. This is the oldest method of enamelling and one which had been brought to perfection by the Chinese; it is the process from which *champlevé* was developed. The design of a piece of *cloisonné* work is formed by the soldering of fine wire, often gold or silver, to a metal base. The series of wells, or cloisons, formed are then filled with enamel. The quality of *cloisonné* work is judged by the number of cloisons per square inch. A demi-tasse cup and saucer that I know has over 4,000 cloisons.

Cloisonné buttons are rare, with the exception of tourist items from modern Japan. Buttons made by this method normally have the reverse side also coated with enamel in order to ease the strain on the base metal and prevent fracturing during cooling. All *cloisonné* articles require careful handling as they are damaged comparatively easily and are not repairable.

Emaux peints (painted enamels). This process was developed at Limoges in France during the fifteenth century, but today all painted enamels are often erroneously referred to as Limoges. In the same way only a tiny proportion of the enamelled boxes etc, now referred to as Battersea ware, were ever made in that location. No buttons have ever been authenticated as coming from Battersea, but apparently some were listed in a bankruptcy sale there in 1856.

The dome shape of these buttons is built up with layers of enamel, each being polished before the next is applied, and finally a design of flowers or figures is painted using a mixture of paint and enamel powder. The whole is then re-fired and perhaps coated with transparent enamel. Sometimes small pieces of foil are incorporated in the design to add glitter. Sometimes the painting is used in conjunction with other methods, the buttons having a *champlevé* border and a painted centre, or having a painted design over *basse taille* work. Painted enamels are not often seen in a matt finish.

Plate 42 shows some small enamel buttons, including three with a matt finish, lower centre; and some examples of diminutives, possibly made for evening gloves.

Background—Italian quilting on satin.

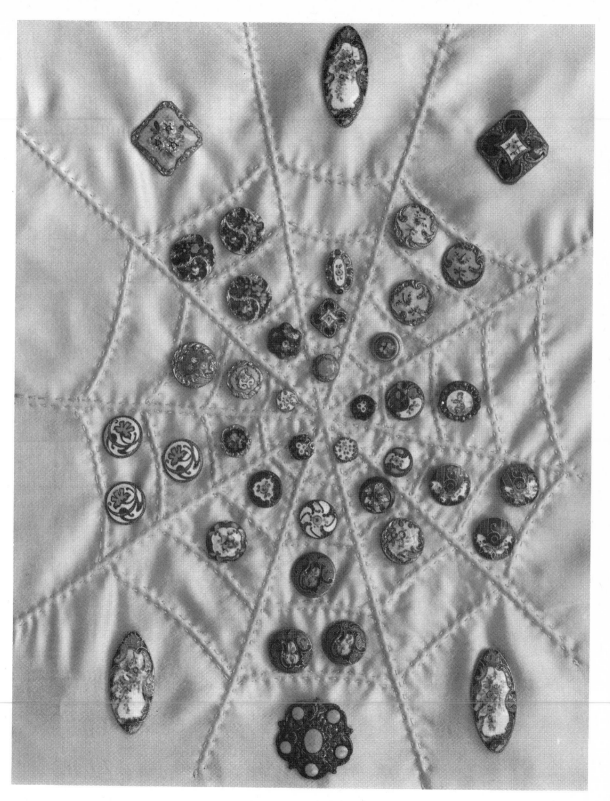

42 *Small enamels and diminutives*   95

Buttons of this type are common and many of them are of poor quality. However, as many fine examples were produced they should not be too hard to find. Plate 41 (see also the frontispiece) shows a good example in the centre, with standing figure and brilliant trim. The floral design with cut steel border represents quality work from the nineteenth century. An example of matt finish can be seen in the second button in the second row. Foil has been incorporated in several of the buttons shown.

En grisaille (pronounced 'on grey sigh'!) This is a method which was developed during the sixteenth century, and in appearance is similar to modern scraper-board work. The background is black, and white enamel and engraving tools are used to produce the design. Buttons made by this method are very scarce.

Encrusting. This is the term used to describe the application of enamel 'beads' which

---

Plate 43 shows a small selection of Paris backs together with three buttons, 11, 12 and 15, known to be from a Paris couture house at the end of the nineteenth century. 12 and 15 are gold plated; 11 is pearl under glass with imitation jewels. The markings are as follows : 1, 2, 3, 4, 5, 6, 8, 10, 14, 17, 'A.P. & Cie'; 7, 'T.W. & W. H.M. Paris Breveté'; 9, 'P & H Paris'; 13, 19, 21, 'T.W. & W.'; 16, 18, 'E.M. Paris'; 20, 'Qualité Solide'.

Background—velvet with Edwardian bead dress trimming.

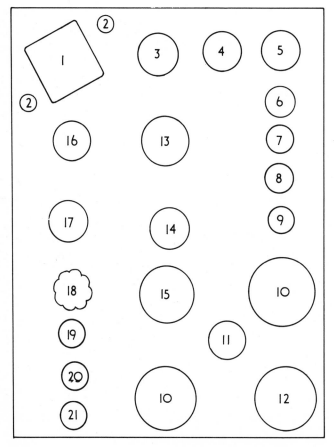

43 *Paris backs and buttons from a couture house*

are found as border decoration for other types of enamel work, or as the sole decoration on metal work of other varieties. The purpose of enamel encrusting was to imitate jewels. The bottom button in plate 42 demonstrates this method clearly.

Paillons. This term is given to small pieces of foil which are placed over several layers of enamel on an engine-turned base and subsequently coated with further enamel. Collectors often refer to them as foil designs, but they should not be confused with cheaper painted enamels incorporating foil.

Pliqué-à-jour. This type of button is rare and fragile. The method used for making them is similar to *cloisonné*, except that there is no base metal. The patterns forming the design are made by soldering wires and filling the spaces like a church window. *The Complete Button Book* and Sally Luscomb's *Collector's Encyclopaedia of Buttons* illustrate examples.

Paris Backs

Originally a Paris back was a button made by the firm of Trelon, Weldon & Weil, a leading Paris house during the nineteenth century. More recently, any buttons marked Paris or bearing the initials of a recognized French house have been called Paris backs. They are much desired by American collectors, initially because they are known to be of good quality, but more recently because they have been 'written up' and have become a fad. The term is generally confined to metal buttons, excluding enamels (plate 43).

T.W. & W. is of course the most sought-after marking, but the one most frequently seen is A.P. & Cie, which is the mark of the firm Albert Parent & Company. Other marks include P.H. Paris (Parent & Hamet, who later became A.P. & Cie), Industrie Parisienne, J.B.M. Paris, H.M. Paris, Paris Breveté and E.M. Paris.

Small Chinas

These fascinating little buttons have become the centre of intense collector interest in America. A book, *Guidelines for Collecting China Buttons,* has been written by members of the National Button Society of America, and a great deal of research into the various patterns has been carried out. Unfortunately the lists of patterns etc are of purely collector origin and do not relate to manufacture, so that they are of little use to British people. All American writers have the great disadvantage of living at least 4,000 miles from the best sources of research, so it is not surprising that confusion of terms arises.

Porcelain buttons made from wet clay were known in France during the eighteenth century, and in Britain they may have been made at Liverpool and transfer-decorated. Wedgwood also produced jasperware button medallions. These, however, are not the buttons now known as small chinas, which were made by a different process, from *dry* clay and pressed out almost in the manner of biscuits. This process was invented in about 1840 by a Birmingham man named Richard Prosser, and was sold to Mr Herbert Minton, who at that time was trading with a partner named Boyle. The firm, now Mintons Ltd, was then Minton & Boyle. It is thought that Prosser was at one time an employee.

The small buttons produced were mainly white ones and were named agates and carnelians; agates were made from earthenware and carnelians from china or porcelain.

Plate 44 shows a selection of the various types of small chinas purchased in America, and white china buttons from British boxes.

Background—a patchwork made from contemporary calico prints of the type these buttons were made to complement.

44   *Small chinas*

In 1949 some reorganization at the Minton works led to the discovery of a quantity of these buttons, including one decorated one, under floorboards. When questioned recently the firm was without a museum curator, but the managing director, Mr J. E. Hartill, told me that in 1846, the last year of manufacture, 50,500 gross buttons were produced.

In the year 1845 production of the white buttons commenced at Worcester under the direction of W. Chamberlain & Company. At that time the Worcester factories, making a variety of items including lavatory pans and ceramic tiles, were at their lowest ebb. The production of the buttons was not considered a commercial success, and shortly after 1850 was abandoned. However, a study of the company's records for 1848-9 shows that the buttons made a profit of £1,950 ($4,680), and that sales totalling approximately £3,000 ($7,200) were made to nearly thirty firms. The records of a few of these firms were investigated for me by the Birmingham Reference Library and it was found that they were button makers and not wholesale drapers, as might have been expected. They included Mr Banks of the Parade, Hammond & Turner, and John Jackson.

At the Dyson Perrins Museum, now part of the Royal Worcester Porcelain Company, there are some examples of buttons: small white china ones mounted on green and blue cards, marked agates and carnelians, and another card containing a few with pink cross-hatching. These latter were donated by a descendant of Robert Chamberlain.

Whether Richard Prosser, the inventor of the process, moved from Mintons to Worcester is open to doubt, but it is known that his brother Thomas emigrated to America and commenced button making there. Thomas filed his own patents and, it appears, later did his best to discredit Richard. At about the same time an enterprising Frenchman by the name of Felix Bapertrosses came to England and obtained employment, probably at Worcester, making buttons. Having learned the secrets of the trade he returned to his native land and, with help from the French government, set up a china-button plant at Braire. He managed to produce the buttons at half the cost of the English ones and, as a result, the English trade collapsed during the 1850s. Unfortunately the English failed to learn their lesson and continued to trust the French. The firm of Bapertrosses is still in business, and was responsible for the production of millions of small china buttons, including those known to collectors as calicoes. I can find no evidence of calicoes, ginghams or other patterned buttons being mass-produced in England, though a few plain-coloured ones are known, in addition to the coloured ones mentioned above. There may have been some American production, and later types of stencil patterns have been found in boxes marked Czechoslovakia which dates them as post-1918.

Calicoes and other small china buttons were underglaze-decorated to stimulate calico material, popular at the time, and are often delightful. It is said in America that the farm women bought cloth for their dresses at the weekly market and at the same time would obtain matching buttons.

The buttons from the firm of Bapertrosses were displayed on folded salesmen's cards with a heading in French. This translated reads: 'All buttons carry a label with the initials F.B. and are made under patented processes'. An example of such a card can be seen at Birmingham Museum, although how it got there is uncertain. The Dyson Perrins Museum has several similar cards, which the curator, Mr H. Sandon, believes to be buttons of Worcester manufacture. In view of other research into the subject, however, and the scarcity of the buttons in England, I am bound to disagree with him. A photograph of the sample card under discussion and another of a card bearing carnelian buttons made at Worcester are reproduced on plate 45, by kind permission of the museum trustees. They were taken by John Beckerley.

100

45 *French sample card and a card
of carnelian buttons*

The buttons shown on the lower left of the sample card are known as ginghams, and again purport to be made to match contemporary fabrics. Specialization in china-button collecting is well established in America, but for the benefit of British readers who might find examples in Europe, some of the collector terms are explained below in greater detail than is possible in the glossary at the back of this book.

COLLECTOR TERMS FOR SMALL CHINAS

Small china - a small button made of clay by the dry pressed process

Calico - a button printed with a calico pattern

Gingham - a button printed with a gingham pattern

Stencil - a button printed with a stencil design and normally later in date than calicoes or ginghams

Oval eye - a two-hole button, the holes being in an oval-shaped depression

Dish type - a button that in cross-section resembles a saucer

Inkwell - a button in section resembling an old school inkpot

Rimmed - a china button with a metal rim

Hobnail - a button with a circle of raised dots round the edge

Jewelled - a button with a fancy metal rim, imitating studding

Pie-crust - a button with a tyre or pie-crust edging; this family has many subdivisions

Gaiter	-	a small chunky china button with a metal loop shank; there are several varieties

Smock	-	a flat overall button with a pin-head shank
Birdcage	-	a four-way shanked button, entirely ceramic
China whistle	-	a button having a single vertical hole at the top and two or more holes at the back
Igloo	-	a hideous-looking object which I imagine was originally made as a practical joke, and one which some Americans have taken very seriously. Collectors coined the name, and pay up to $48 (£20) a time. It is a flat china disk with a stud-like lump on the top and is threaded by a series of complicated twists. Nothing is known about its history, but every serious American collector has to have one!

Those interested in making a study of china buttons are referred to current American publications. Personally I consider calicoes to be quite charming, and only regret that they are not seen in Britain.

Satsumas

Satsuma, a province in Kyushu, the southern island of Japan, has given its name to a distinctive type of pottery which has been produced since the fifteenth century. Satsuma ware was originally developed by the Koreans in an attempt to copy Chinese porcelain, but during the fifteenth century a prince of Satsuma invaded Korea and brought back prisoners who subsequently made the pottery in Japan. In the nineteenth and twentieth centuries the old wares have been much copied and exported. Satsuma buttons are being made currently for export to America.

Old Satsuma is made of fine white clay and when finished has the appearance of old ivory. The glaze is intentionally crackled by a process developed in the sixteenth century. The decoration of old Satsuma is fine and delicate and involves the use of much gold stippling together with the discreet use of other colours on the characteristic cream ground. Satsuma buttons were not made before the middle of the nineteenth century; the earliest were of the finest quality. They show typical Japanese scenes or portraits and are usually self-shanked. Other small items such as brooches, buckles and hatpin tops were also made, primarily for export.

As a collector's item Satsuma buttons are highly desirable. Their beauty and workmanship alone deserve admiration. Large quantities of modern ones are available in the

USA and even these are worth having, provided a price distinction is made!

In Britain, Satsuma buttons are relatively scarce, the majority having been brought back by missionaries and other travellers, including my aunt Mrs F. H. Easton, who lent me the three hexagonal ones shown on plate 46.

Hardstone Buttons

The production of buttons from a variety of precious, semi-precious and other stones, ranging from diamonds to polished beach pebbles, has been carried out for many years. W. C. Aitkin, writing on the Birmingham button trade, tells of real stone buttons being cut with a lapidary's slicer and the cut fawcetted and polished. They were perforated by the use of a copper drill. At the time of the Great Exhibition in 1851, button blanks made from carnelian and other stones were imported from Bohemia to be shanked and finished in Birmingham, Neal & Tonks being the only British firm listed as manufacturing them. Today commercial production of stone buttons has apparently ceased in Britain, though amateur craft workshops produce a limited number. In the April 1970 edition of the *Lapidary Journal*, American readers were given instructions on amateur stone button making.

The hardstone buttons which the collector is most likely to come across are those made from members of the quartz family. Quartz, one of the most common minerals of the earth's crust, forms an important part of most igneous rocks (ie those formed by the action of fire, as opposed to the sedimentary rocks which were formed by the action of water).

Quartz is found in crystals of varying qualities and colours, the most common types in the gemstone range being:

rock crystal	-	transparent and clear
rose quartz	-	pink
blue quartz	-	blue
citrine	-	yellow
amethyst	-	purple and mauve
smoky quartz or cairngorm	-	smoky yellow, orange, brown

Chalcedony is translucent quartz and contains microscopic crystals. It is known as:

agate	-	a wide variety of colours and irregular bandings
onyx	-	more regular banding of black, white and brown
carnelian or sard	-	almost clear reddish brown
jasper	-	opaque, red, yellow or brown
bloodstone	-	opaque, red and green

One difficulty is in differentiating between hardstone and glass buttons, or those made from synthetic stones. Many manufacturers used to deliberately imitate stones in glass. As a very quick guide the following may help:

hardness	-	quartz is harder than glass and will scratch it
coldness	-	minerals are usually colder and heavier than glass

---

The nineteenth-century Satsuma buttons shown on plate 46 have self-shanks.
Background—hemstitching on linen.

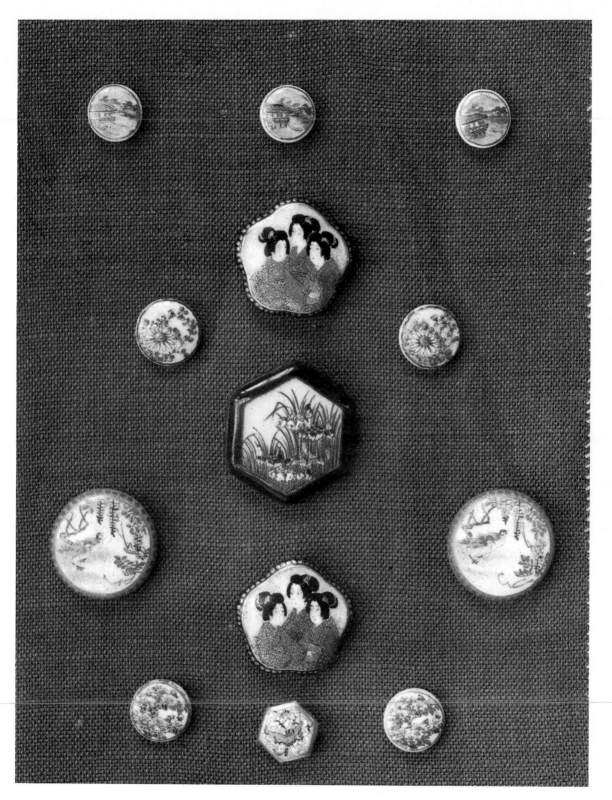

46 *Nineteenth-century Satsuma buttons*

clarity	when viewed against a strong light, minerals tend to show their crystalline structure and impurities; even, regular patterning is suspect

There is no connection at all between hardstone buttons and the small chinas known as agates and carnelians. Why the names were adopted for the china buttons is unknown, but they are likely to confuse the ignorant—yet another reason for never buying buttons without seeing them first. If in doubt over stone buttons, ask a jeweller to test them.

Eighteenth-century stone buttons were usually flat polished disks with a pin-head, like the one shown on the frontispiece (this was lent by Mrs K. Taylor). The shank is silver; those on plate 47 are later in date and have steel shanks. Pieces of semi-precious stone were also used as the centres of two-piece metal buttons, in which case the mounts were of better material and quality than those used for glass (see section on the Luckock collection).

In the nineteenth century and later, pin-head shanks were used, but a more common method was partial drilling and insertion of a shank and back plate. Modern amateur buttons are cemented to a back plate with epoxy resin. Ball and dome-shaped buttons were made for men's waistcoats, but at the beginning of this century ladies wore them on blouses. Queen Victoria's love of Balmoral Castle and tartan outfits trimmed with the work of Scottish craftsmen, encouraged the production of stone buttons in Scotland.

Diminutives

This is another collector term, and like others has come from America. It refers to any button which will pass through a hole $\frac{3}{8}$in in diameter.

Collectors refer to buttons which will pass through a $\frac{3}{4}$in hole as small, those up to $1\frac{1}{2}$in as medium, and those larger than that as large. The National Button Society is responsible for this terminology and issues small gauges to collectors for measuring buttons. It is a pity they did not co-ordinate their thinking with the manufacturers, who measure their buttons in 'lines'. In 1853 a Mr Perkins wrote a small book entitled *A Treatise on Haberdashery*, and in 1874 a revised edition was published. The purpose of this work was to educate small shopkeepers and their assistants in the ways of the haberdasher and to prevent them falling on hard times through poor stock-keeping. The 1874 edition discusses the measurement of buttons as follows:

> Pearl shirt buttons are made in various patterns designated severally plain, cup, figured, bevil ring cup, ring bevil, fish eye, flat and fancy. Their size as well as other buttons is determined by an admeasurement with a gauge, and they are known as 12 line, 14 line, going up by regular intervals to 24 line, the size increasing with the numerical value. The term line signifies the fortieth part of an inch, the button being measured across the diameter to furnish its numerical value.

Plate 47 shows a selection of hardstone buttons. At the top is a white chalcedony button with gilt mount. In row 2 are 3 carved agates with pinhead shanks. Row 3 has a jasper ball, 2 turquoise chips in pinchbeck (Persian), an amethyst in silver mount, and a conglomerate ball button.

Row 4 has a sardonyx at each end and an agate in the centre. Row 5 shows two lozenge-shaped carnelians at each end; in the centre and in row 6 are agates. In row 7 is a small petalite ball; and in row 8 a set of 6 carnelian buttons from Scotland.

Background—sandpaper.

106

47 *Hardstone buttons*

This book also gives a diagram showing sizes from 10 to 36 lines.

It is no doubt a matter of pure coincidence that in Birmingham in 1850 there was a gentleman by the name of Lines, who at that time was over eighty, but still employed as an engraver of button dies. He was responsible for the discovery and training of the majority of designers employed in the industry and for the production of most original designs.

One line equals 1/40th or 25thou of an inch. The following table will enable readers to measure the buttons they find. For the benefit of American readers, buttons of 14 lines or less are diminutives, 15-29 small, 30-59 medium and 60 and over are large. British collectors will probably find it easier to use these manufacturing measurements.

1/8 inch	=	5 lines		1 inch	=	40 lines
1/4 ,,	=	10 ,,	1	1/8 ,,	=	45 ,,
3/8 ,,	=	15 ,,	1	1/4 ,,	=	50 ,,
1/2 ,,	=	20 ,,	1	3/8 ,,	=	55 ,,
5/8 ,,	=	25 ,,	1	1/2 ,,	=	60 ,,
3/4 ,,	=	30 ,,	1	5/8 ,,	=	65 ,,
7/8 ,,	=	35 ,,				

There is a French method of measuring buttons, also using the term 'lines', but it is now rarely met, and does not coincide with the British method—naturally!

Diminutive buttons are worth collecting on their own merit, as there is such a wide range available. Many of the sizes will never be repeated as in this age of machine-made goods and zip fasteners they are obsolete. However, doll dressers find them invaluable, and many pretty objects can be decorated with them. In monetary terms they are worth less than similar larger buttons.

Wooden Buttons

Wood was probably the material used by cavemen to make a primitive toggle to hold their skins in place, but wooden buttons as we know them have mostly been made during the last 150 years. Due to the relative softness of the material, its rapid deterioration in water, and the fact that a wooden button is primarily functional as opposed to decorative, few earlier examples exist.

Wooden buttons were made in several places in Britain during the nineteenth century, and wooden moulds for covering were turned out by the million. There was also a short-lived craze during the 1930s for large wooden buttons. Some had the appearance of cross-sections cut from small logs and in my opinion were decidedly ugly. The 1970 edition of *Kompass* listed six companies producing wooden buttons, but a quick survey of stores in the west end of London that year did not produce any examples of British manufacture. In the Republic of Ireland wooden buttons are currently made in Dublin and sold for home knitters to use with Aran wools. This is carrying on an Irish tradition for such items, as in 1851 William Griffiths, an inventor and manufacturer of Grafton Street, Dublin, exhibited a variety of small items, including buttons, at the Great Exhibition. These were made from bog oak, which is a semi-petrified wood excavated

---

Diminutive buttons shown on plate 48 include items made from the following materials: glass, painted metal, silver, lustre glass, brass, plated metal, vegetable ivory, enamel, celluloid, pearl, leather, plastic.
Background—1930s modesty vest!

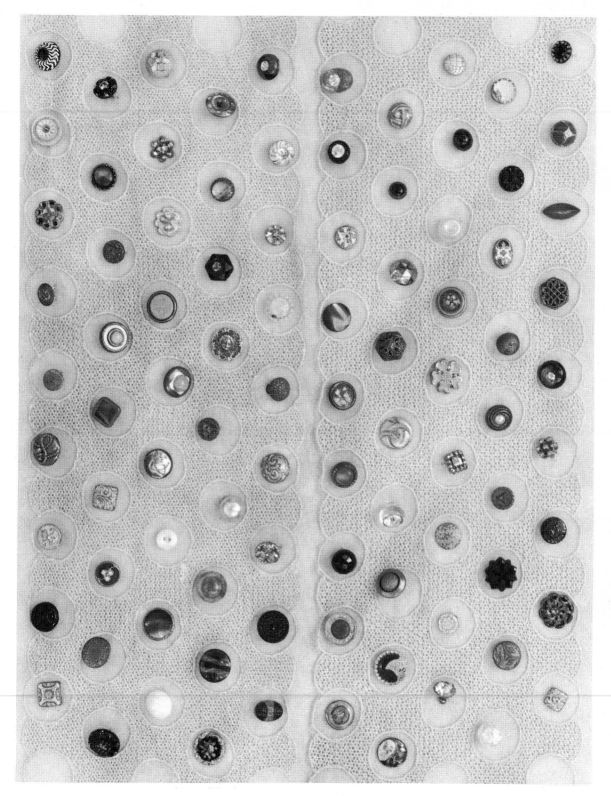

48 *Diminutives*

from Irish bogs. Bog oak is black and resembles ebony. Like jet and black vulcanite it was popular during court mourning. It is of interest to note that the Pinto collection of treen (woodenware) at present housed in Birmingham Museum does not contain any example of Tunbridge-ware buttons; nor is reference made to buttons of this type at the Great Exhibition. In America, however, 'Tunbridge' buttons are made in California!

During the nineteenth century American buttons were turned from a variety of woods—apple, yew and box being popular. Benjamin Randolph, a well-known cabinet-maker, was noted for them. Contemporary British sources mentioned beech or box as the commonest varieties and stated that buttons from the woods were turned, polished and varnished. Better-class buttons were made from ebony, rosewood and walnut.

Wood has of course been used for button making in conjunction with many other materials, including pearl, metal, barbola and fabrics. Wooden moulds formed the base for the Leek buttons and for French crochet-work buttons. The softness of the material allows for inlay, carving and embossing to be easily carried out.

Buttons from around the World

The button is a universal object, and in its present form originated in the Middle East. Persians were wearing buttons at a time when the British still decorated themselves with woad and America was an undiscovered jungle.

It is quite impossible to classify every specimen of button, and those who try are defeating the main object of collecting. A hobby that began as a pleasure becomes a chore if one becomes rigid in thought and application. The arranging of buttons is as interesting as the finding of them, and it takes far longer than one imagines. When I was working on this book I found that few of the plate settings could be done in less than two or three hours, excluding the working of the backgrounds.

American collectors mount their buttons in picture-type frames, and there are persons who make and sell accessories for the purpose. They usually use cream card grounds, and find the idea of sewing or knitting a background amusing. As one lady told me, 'All you British do in your spare time is sew, knit or walk about in the rain!' Yet buttons were made to be associated with fabrics and so to me it seems natural to mount them on fabric grounds. Choosing and working a suitable ground is interesting, and frames of buttons mounted in this way make good conversation pieces and are a change from the reproduction Constable or sampler.

––––––––––

In the top row of plate 49 are examples of fish designs cut from coconut shell. Such buttons are made for tourists in the Caribbean and other areas. In the centre of the top row is a lacquered and gilded wooden button with loop shank—a good example of nineteenth-century work. Row 2 shows (left and right ends) some partly covered wood moulds, widely sold for home dressmakers, a Chinese hardwood button and tassel knob, from a nineteenth-century costume brought back by a missionary, and in the centre a wooden base with heavy barbola trimming—although loop-shanked as a button, this was found as a hat trimming.

Row 3 shows some wooden buttons from Dublin, 1970, and three more are below. In row 4, 2nd left, is an ebony button inlaid with pearl shell; then a wooden button, c 1930, with plastic chips in the fixative. In row 5 is a small grey-painted engine-turned button and 4 examples of 1930s types. Row 6 shows painted wooden buttons, purchased from workshops for the blind, and a wooden mould home-covered with satin and tatting, West of England work.

Background—moss-stitch knitting in Aran wool.

110

49 *Wooden buttons*

50 *Metal buttons*

Apart from formal display and use on clothing, collectors' buttons can also be used to decorate collage work, mosaics or, in the case of plastic buttons, to cover jars and lamp bases. Old and valuable buttons should not of course be stuck down or mutilated.

Heads and Tales

Many American collectors arrange their buttons in the way philatelists arrange their stamps: they group all those of one pictorial type together. American books tend to show buttons arranged in this way rather than by historical or manufacturing divisions.

Among such classifications that of 'Heads' ranks high. It is regarded with as much interest as metal pictures. Many buttons were made with portrait heads as a design, sometimes for a specific purpose, but often just as a representation of a pretty girl. Male heads are rare, except in the political campaign category. The Art Nouveau period is particularly remembered by its heads—the flowing locks of female hair could be used to advantage by the designers. Perhaps the seventies will produce unisex heads?

Livery Buttons

The study of livery buttons and uniform buttons (next section) could form a subject for an entire book, and one which I feel to be outside my scope. British collectors of such buttons are often men interested in militaria, and to do this job properly one needs to be well informed on military history, heraldry and other subjects. However, it is necessary to mention these buttons briefly, as they complete the pattern of button making from 1800 to 1940.

Livery buttons were made to adorn the uniforms of servants and others in the employ of the aristocracy, but later personalized devices of all kinds were also used on civilian outfits. Many firms have been associated with the production of livery buttons over the years, but some of the names that appear on the backs are merely those of distributors or wholesale tailors. The oldest firm is Firmin & Sons Ltd, who commenced business during the reign of Charles II. J. R. Gaunt & Sons Ltd and C. Pitt & Co are two other well-known names.

At the end of the 1950s some Americans visited Britain and purchased from Firmins a large number of old sample books containing thousands of buttons. These were shipped to the States and sold to collectors. Five complete books are now in the Just

---

On plate 50 is a small selection of metal buttons from a wide variety of sources. In the top corners are two plated buttons based on a horse-chestnut-leaf design. In the top centre is a French metal button with enamel encrustations. Rows 2 and 3 show a set of seven buttons decorated with niello work, from the Middle East. Row 4 has four open-work silver buttons, from Holland or Brittany. In row 5 are four hollow silver buttons from Spain, and in the centre an example of Japanese metal work (lent by Mrs F. J. Andrews). Row 6 shows a Dutch or Italian hollow Sheffield-plated button, and some modern niello work from Bangkok. Row 7 shows oyster-shell buttons—probably British or French— and a small metal ball from the tribal costume of the Yeo people in North Thailand. These people, now living in the mountains adjoining Burma, originally came from southern China, but—like the Tibetans—on moving to a warmer climate they failed to adapt their mode of dress. They wear heavy dark cloth trousers and jackets, similar to a judo outfit but heavily embroidered, and thick turbans.

The small buttons round the lower edge of the plate are stamped with Arabic writing and appear to have been cut from coins or some other article. Loop shanks have been attached.

Background—hand-knitting.

The two top rows on plate 51 illustrate the category of Heads, the button at the top right-hand corner showing a portrait of Sarah Bernhardt. The other buttons are a miscellaneous selection and include some of the oddities that a collector gathers over a period. In the border are some of the smallest pearl buttons I have found. I had difficulty in getting a needle small enough to sew them on.

1, representation (in metal) of a walnut; 2, three carved ivory monkey faces from a set of six, marked 'Made in Japan'; 3, barrel-shaped button trimmed with enamel, from China; 4, 'Jones Parade Leicester'—small brass button, probably from a firm's uniform though a local search failed to produce information, and made by C.E.A. & Sons, Birmingham; 5, traditional square button from Scottish Highland dress—the 2 lozenge thistle below were also for this purpose, and all were made by Buttons Ltd; 6, 'You Liar' —a curiosity obtained in Cornwall, its back being inscribed 'Go to Davis Gooch St Birmingham for guinea gold wedding rings' : to date no one has been able to trace this firm or offer suggestions as to the uses of such buttons—perhaps they were presented to prospective bridegrooms !

7, the square button with floral motif is from the 1920s, and the engraved dress-shirt button next to it, 8, was made by Sherlock & Co, Covent Garden; 9, 'Never Ripum' is a typical example of an American work-clothes button, such buttons were produced by the million and carried a variety of slogans—most blue-collar workers in the States wear some kind of uniform, clean and smart ! 10, to the British a ladybird, to Americans a goofy ladybug—milk-glass button from children's wear of the 1930s; 11, small brass button, lacquered in the style of Pontypool, South Wales—nineteenth century; 12, croquet was a popular game with the country gentry from 1880 onwards—this button,

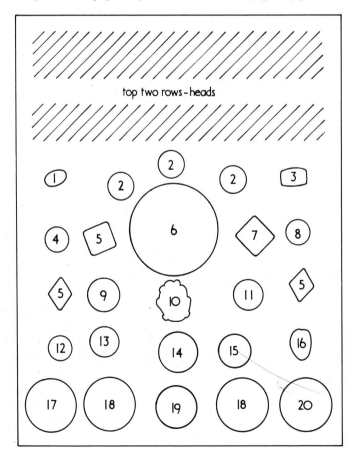

top two rows – heads

51 *'Heads' and a collector's miscellany*

which is also known in black, carries croquet motifs, and at the back the diamond registration mark, a fairly scarce feature.

13, the golf ball is marked Dunlop 65 and may be a key-ring decoration, not a button —a similar decoration often mistaken for a button is a Heinz cucumber; 14, embossed leatherwork; 15, the blackcurrant button, which caused much amusement in America where apparently their cultivation is banned due to some disease; 16, button made from a cowrie shell with soldered shank; 17, a perspex button from the 1930s; 18, two modern American copies of eighteenth-century buttons known as tombacs, these being made of white metal and bought recently in Philadelphia; 19, the moon landing!—this button was made for the 1970 dress trade, but was being sold to collectors by the Colorado State Button Club, which gave me one for inclusion in this book; 20, the last button is made from tortoiseshell inlaid with silver—another example of this work, which is rare, is found on the frontispiece; such buttons have been recently imitated in plastic.

Background—card.

Buttons Museum; the others are scattered. Consequently the American demand for such buttons has dropped, and most of those purchased now are for tailors to use on blazers. The Duke's livery buttons go well with the Old Etonian tie from Miami Beach!

The buttons shown on plate 52 are chosen from the many available, those with birds and animals being picked for general interest. The Borough of Penzance button in the centre is marked on the back 'R. Pearce Mayor 1838', and is interesting as it was singled out in 1909 by Mr R. L. B. Rathbone as being a good example of a decorative municipal button. Local enquiries produced the information that the old Cornish name for the town was Pen Zans, meaning holy head, and this is the reason why the head of John the Baptist was chosen for the coat of arms.

Mr Rathbone maintained, as other writers have done, that the practice of allowing one's personal crest to appear on the clothing of servants was incorrect. No servant would be allowed, for instance, to wear replicas of his master's medals. The habit of livery buttons, however, which began in the eighteenth century, became a vogue in the nineteenth. The College of Arms probably didn't like it, but it still persists among the nobility.

Those wishing to make a study of livery buttons are referred to *Fairbairn's Book of Crests of the Families of Great Britain and Ireland*, but are warned that it is a long and difficult procedure to identify particular crests correctly.

Civic buttons are easier to identify as most borough councils have good archives (but they may not welcome the attentions of collectors).

Uniform Buttons

Articles on uniform buttons have appeared in British magazines, and military museums provide more information. In 1907 a book entitled *The Heritage of Dress* by W. M. Webb gave much interesting history on the subject of button positions. Many of these derive from the days of horse riding, and those on the uniform of pageboys derive from Dutch skeleton dress, originally indicating ribs.

Another interesting fact disclosed in this work is that the regiments in the Brigade of Guards in the British Army may be distinguished by the arrangement of their tunic

---

Plate 52 shows a selection of livery buttons.
Background—corded velvet fabric, from Harrods of Knightsbridge.

52 *Livery buttons*

buttons. Those of the Grenadiers are evenly spaced, the Coldstreams in pairs, the Scots in threes and the Irish Guards in fours. Mr Webb also refers to Quakers who refused to wear metal buttons!

In America uniforms and their buttons have long been a subject for study, once again with a strong male element. The Civil War provided much interesting material, as do the buttons from various State military organizations. Uniforms are popular in America, except for schoolchildren, who find the British custom of school uniform odd.

The buttons shown on plate 53 are a small sample from the thousands of uniform buttons available. They are listed with the names of their makers or distributors.

In the top row, left to right: Devonshire Police, one of the many British county police forces (now amalgamated with Cornwall), 'Buttons Ltd'; British Army issue, World War II, 'W.L.M. Ltd Birmingham'; British Royal Navy, World War II, 'Firmins'; British Royal Air Force, World War II, 'Buttons Ltd'; Somerset Police, c 1950 (now Somerset and Bath), 'Herbert and Co London'.

Row 2: British Coastguard Service, unmarked; Air Raid Precautions (British civilian war organization), unmarked; Civil Defence (voluntary British civilian defence organization recently disbanded), 'H & H Birmingham'; Auxiliary Fire Service (British), World War II, 'Ed Gill Birmingham'; General Post Office (British), pre-1939, 'Buttons Ltd'.

Row 3: The Devonshire Regiment, 'Hawkes and Co Piccadilly'; Prince Albert's, Somerset Regiment, c 1870, 'Special quality'; South Devon Militia, c 1890, 'Firmins'; Royal Army Ordnance Corps (British), 'Firmins'; Lancashire Yeomanry, 'Firmins'.

Row 4: Dublin Fusiliers, pre-1920, 'Henecy and Sons, Dublin'; London & South Western Railway, 'Buttons Ltd'; Great Western Railway, 'J. Compton Sons & Webb, London'; Taff Vale Railway, South Wales (all railways in Britain were nationalized in 1947), 'J. Compton Sons & Webb'; Irish Rifles, pre-1920, 'Hawkes'.

Row 5: New Zealand Combined Forces, World War II, 'Gaunts'; Royal Artillery, 'Stillwell & Co London'; Canadian Women's Air Corps, 'United Carr, Canada'; Langham Hotel (now the headquarters of the British Broadcasting Corporation), 'Buttons Ltd'; British Merchant Navy, 'Gaunts'.

Row 6: Lincolnshire Regiment, 'Jennens & Co London'; Royal Corps of Signals, 'Buttons Ltd'; Lord Lieutenant (chief executive authority and head of magistracy in British county), 'Charles Smith, Piccadilly'; Great Southern & Western Railway, Ireland, unmarked; Cork & Bandon Railway, Ireland, 'Firmins'.

Row 7: Cheshire Regiment, 'Buttons Ltd'; Somerset Light Infantry, 'Turner Bros, Bath'; London, Midland & Scottish Railway, 'Buttons Ltd'; Manchester Corporation Transport (municipal buses), unmarked; British Railways, 'Gaunts'; United States Services, World War II, 'Superior quality'; 55th Border Regiment, unmarked (I am told by the dealer in militaria who assisted with the identification of all these buttons that the connection with China is purely historical!)

Background—uniform fabric.

53 *Uniform buttons*

PRACTICAL HINTS FOR COLLECTORS

Those who have been collecting buttons for some time or who have friends who do so, will know how to go about it and how to arrange them. These hints are for beginners.

HOW TO START COLLECTING

One collects buttons as one collects anything else, firstly by learning about them and secondly by gathering them. If the process is done in reverse the collection is no more than a hoard.

Most collectors will find buttons in the family button-box which will be useful for purposes of identification. This may be a source of some good buttons if it has been in the house for more than thirty years. Friends, relatives and auctions will produce more buttons. With reference to auctions, it is wise to remember that most button tins are worth 50p ($1.20), but few are worth more than that unless one knows the contents.

Jumble sales and charity shops are poor sources as most of the clothing is modern. Antique and junk shops are better, but, as stated previously, very few of them know anything about buttons. They price either according to decorative interest or to what they think American tourists will pay. One or two sell to the dress trade.

Collecting old buttons is not an investment, but an interesting hobby. The buttons are unlikely to appreciate in value as silver does, but will give a lot of pleasure to the owner, and provide scope for artistic arrangement.

When purchasing buttons, as with other items, collectors are advised to insist on seeing documentary proof before believing any historical stories in the sales talk. I have lost count of the number of buttons said to have been made especially for Queen Victoria, Queen Mary, Sir Winston Churchill and others, and offered to me at inflated prices. One set purported to come from gaiters worn by the Archbishop of Canterbury. As they carried a Roman Catholic emblem, I thought it a likely tale!

How these stories originate is difficult to say, but the wish is usually father to the thought. A casual remark by someone who once knew someone whose cousin knew someone who was sister of the Queen's maid, is quite enough to start the ball rolling. An attentive audience and the possibility of financial gain are all that is required to expand on the theme.

Buyers are reminded that because a button is old it is not necessarily either rare, valuable or of particular collector merit. I once called on a village tailor to see old button stock and was shown among others numerous small four-hole buttons. When I indicated that they were of no special interest, the man expressed surprise and said, 'But, Miss, these must be good ones, they were a special line my father stocked for the squire's gaiters'. Collectors are particularly warned against buying buttons through any type of general buying-and-selling magazine or newspaper. Such publications often contain a large number of phoney advertisements and attempts to obtain free valuations.

TOOLS AND EQUIPMENT

It is wise to have a box to keep together the following:

pencil, biro and felt-tip pen, tailor's chalk

two pairs of scissors, one good pair and one old pair for cutting florists' wire etc

small pair of wire cutters for cutting pipe cleaners, and straightening bent loop shanks (this must be done gently or they break)

quantity of pipe cleaners cut in fours

reel of fine florists' wire or fine telephone wire with plastic coating

needles and thread

old bristle toothbrush and jewellers' brushes

double-sided adhesive tape

shoemaker's awl or stiletto from old-fashioned sewing box (if unobtainable a small screwdriver can be ground to a point)

You will also need a quantity of card. For preliminary mounting old household cartons, writing-pad backs etc will do. Use a tea tray for a working surface. Buttons roll about and table tops become scratched.

CHOOSING AND SORTING

If buttons are in a box or tin, turn them out on a tray or large plate and sort into types. Reject any that are chipped, badly scratched or rusty. Bent shanks can be straightened, but built-up backs and four-way shanks cannot be repaired if broken. Two- and four-way shanks are sometimes squashed flat and it is very difficult to open them out. Steel buttons cannot be cleaned once they have rusted.

CLEANING

Glass, plain pearl, vegetable-ivory and plastic buttons may be carefully washed with warm water and soap (not detergent). Most other buttons should not be washed with water; even if it does not harm the front it may lodge inside and cause rusting. Spirit cleaning fluid may be used carefully with a soft rag or jeweller's brush on buttons made of bone, horn and some types of fabric. Uniform buttons may be cleaned with metal cleaner, but many metal buttons are finished with lacquer or bronzing and must not be so treated. Golden Age buttons, for example, must only be dusted. Most buttons can be improved by rubbing gently with a soft rag, but spirit cleaners must never be allowed to come into contact with gold work, decorated pearls or inlays.

STORING AND ARRANGING

If one has large numbers of buttons they can be stored in glass jars, but as buttons jumbled up together are their own worst enemies it is best to arrange them on cards. For a preliminary period any old card will do. Sew-through types can be attached with wire or double-sided adhesive tape, and shanked buttons are pushed through a hole and secured with a pipe cleaner or wire. Push the wire through the shank and then twist it back to prevent it slipping out. Watch for rust, and store the buttons in a warm dry place away from direct sunlight. Drawers or old filing cabinets are excellent receptacles.

For final arrangement choose or make a suitable background and lay out the buttons, allowing a border and sufficient fold-over at the edges for attachment to a backing. When satisfied, and it takes time, measure the positions carefully and mark the centre point for each button with tailor's chalk or pencil. Place the buttons on a piece of paper or card in matching positions; they may then be transferred from this and attached one by one

121

to the prepared lay-out. Remember that if the positions have been marked on the reverse side of the background the front will be a mirror image of the arrangement.

The finished mounting should then be set on a stiff card, hardboard or plywood backing. If paper or something similar has been used the edges may be folded over and glued to the back, but most fabric grounds should be secured by needle and thread in the same sort of way as in tapestry work.

Buttons can be mounted in picture frames without glass, though glass is advisable as a protection. American collectors use special glazed frames similar to those used for mounted butterflies, but these are not easily obtainable in Britain as yet.

A personal note

The author regrets that owing to other commitments she is unable to answer general questions on buttons or collecting from private individuals; nor can she make free valuations. Written enquiries from museums, industry and other official sources are welcome on a business basis.

Persons who have buttons they wish to offer for sale or who wish to receive details of any future British business arrangements are requested to send a stamped addressed envelope for a printed notice of business terms. Buttons are offered for sale by mail order in North America and on receipt of an International Reply Coupon a current list will be forwarded to enquirers.

Readers are reminded that the inclusion of any button in the illustrations in this book is not of itself an indication of special value.

METHODS OF ATTACHMENT AND BUTTON BACKS

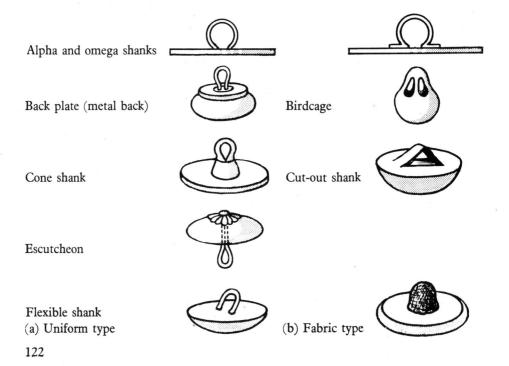

Alpha and omega shanks

Back plate (metal back)   Birdcage

Cone shank   Cut-out shank

Escutcheon

Flexible shank
(a) Uniform type   (b) Fabric type

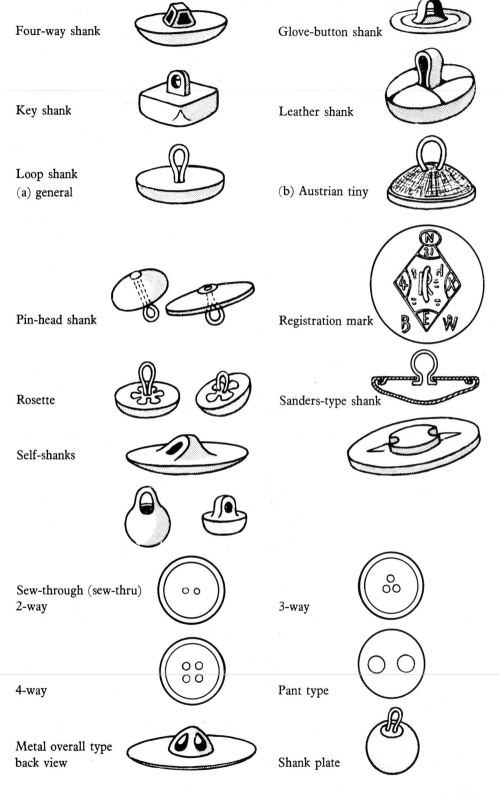

Four-way shank

Glove-button shank

Key shank

Leather shank

Loop shank
(a) general

(b) Austrian tiny

Pin-head shank

Registration mark

Rosette

Sanders-type shank

Self-shanks

Sew-through (sew-thru)
2-way

3-way

4-way

Pant type

Metal overall type
back view

Shank plate

Split shank (19th century pearl types)

Swirl back   Thread back

Turret shank    Two-way shank with thread guide

Wedge shank

GLOSSARY

Many of the terms used both by button manufacturers and by American collectors have been explained in the text of this book, but for quick reference those in most general use are listed below. Terms used in connection with Enamels and Small China buttons have been explained under those headings in the text. Terms used in connection with methods of attachment are listed separately above.

Back mark	Any inscription or trade mark on the back of a button
Ball	A spherical button
Beaded button	A passementerie type trimmed with beads
Breveté	French term for patented

Bull's eye	Small china button marked in circular rings
Button mould	Piece of bone, wood or metal for covering with thread or fabric
Buttony	Name used in Dorset for button making
Calico	*see* section on Small Chinas
Campaign button	Made for political campaigns in USA
Carnelian	(a) Type of small china button
	(b) Variety of hardstone
Casein	Plastic substance made from milk
Celluloid	First type of plastic material
Champlevé	*see* section on Enamels

Charm string	String of 1,000 buttons
Cloisonné	*see* section on Enamels
Collet	A metal rim holding a jewel in place
Colonial	Eighteenth-century American button
Corozo	Nut from which vegetable-ivory buttons are made
Cut steel	Steel facets
Déposé	French term meaning registered trademark
Diminutive	American term for button under $\frac{3}{8}$in in diameter

Drum	Thick straight-sided button
Emaux peints	*see* section on Enamels
Escutcheon	Decorative method of trimming button fronts
Filigree	Lace-like metal work

Fish eye	Manufacturers' name for two-hole button with oval depression surrounding the holes
Forbidden money	American name for imitation coin buttons
Freshwater pearl	Shell of river mollusc
Gaiter	*see* section on Small Chinas
Gingham	*see* section on Small Chinas
Golden Age	1800-1850
Goofy	American name for an oddly shaped modern button; usually made of plastic
Hallmark	Quality mark stamped on articles made of silver and gold
Igloo	American joke—*see* section on Small Chinas
Inaugural	American button made for presidential inauguration
Inkwell	*see* section on Small Chinas
Iridescent	Rainbow-effect finish on glass
Ivoroid	*see* Celluloid
Jewel	American name for button with large stone in centre
Jewelled	Button with many pieces of glass trim
Kaleidoscope	Multi-coloured glass button
Lacy	Variety of pressed-glass button made in Bohemia
Line	25thou or 1/40th of an inch. Manufacturers' button measurement
Link button	Similar to a cape fastening
Lithograph	Photograph or picture button
Locket button	Rare type of button used by military spies etc; the back unscrews to reveal a compass

Mourning button	Dull black glass button, or one with inlaid white cross
Niello	Method of decorating metal buttons; scratched design is filled with black enamel
Norwalk	American pottery button made in Connecticut
Nut button	Slang name for vegetable-ivory button

Paperweight	Type of glass button
	see section on Ball buttons
Paris back	French button, marked as such
Passementerie	(a) Button covered with beads or braid
	(b) Italian term for dress trimmings
Paste	Glass brilliant
Peacock eye	American name for variety of waistcoat button;
	see section on Waistcoat buttons
Pearl	Button made from pearl shell
Pearlies	London costermongers' clothes decorated with hundreds of small pearl buttons
Pie crust	Serrated edge on small china button
Plastic horn	Moulded horn in use before 1873; no connection with plastic material
Reflector	Mirror-back button; *see* section on Brilliants
Registration mark	Indication of registration of British patent
Satsuma	Japanese pottery button
Sew-through (or Sew-thru)	Button with holes from front to back
Stencil	*see* section on Small Chinas
Studio button	Modern reproduction; mainly American
Suspender button	American name for trouser button to attach braces
Tagua palm	Alternative source of vegetable ivory
Velvet back	*see* section on Fabric buttons
Vest button	American name for a waistcoat button

| Whistle | *see* section on Small Chinas. |
| Zodiac | Set of buttons, mainly modern, depicting the signs of the zodiac, popular in America |

BIBLIOGRAPHY

ACLAND, J. E. 'Dorset Buttony', *Dorset Natural History and Antiquarian Field Club Proceedings* 1914

ADAMS, John. 'Potters Parade', *Pottery and Glass* 1951

AITKEN, W. C. 'Buttons', *British Manufacturing Industries* 1876

The Art Journal 1862

Birmingham Assizes 1800 (E. Piercey, Printer, Bull St, Birmingham)

BLACKER, J. F. *Chats on Oriental China* 1908

BOTT and CLEPHANE. *Our Mothers 1870-1900* 1932

BRADBURY, F. *Guide to Marks of Origin on British and Irish Silver Plate* (J. W. Northend, Sheffield) 1959

'The Button Manufacture of Birmingham', *The Illustrated Exhibitor and Magazine of Art* 1852

CHAMBERLAIN and MINER. *Button Heritage* (Heritage Press NY) 1967

COPE, G. F. 'Pearl Buttons', *British Buttons* May/June 1947

CUNNINGTON, C. Willet. *Feminine Attitudes in the Nineteenth Century* 1936

'The Dyeing of Buttons', *Imperial Chemical Industries Technical Circular* 1945

English Historic Costumes Nos 13-16 (Windsor and Newton, painting books)

Fairbairn's Book of Crests of the Families of Great Britain and Ireland (1905)

FOSTER-BROWN, D. *Button Parade* (Mid-America Book Co) 1968

GIBBS SMITH, C. H. *The Fashionable Lady in the Nineteenth Century* (Victoria & Albert Museum, London) 1960

GODDEN, G. *Encyclopaedia of British Pottery and Porcelain Marks* (Crown Publishers, NY) 1964

Great Exhibition 1851. Official Descriptive & Illustrated Catalogue

Guidelines for Collecting China Buttons (National Button Society of America) 1970

HILLIER, B. *Art Deco* (Studio Vista) 1970

History and Description of the Great Exhibition 1851 Vol 3 (London Printing and Publishing Co)

Just Buttons Magazine 1967-70 (Southington, Connecticut)

KOCH, R. *Louis C. Tiffany—Rebel in Glass* (Crown Publishers NY)

LUSCOMB, Sally. *The Collector's Encyclopaedia of Buttons* (Crown Publishers NY)

NOVINGER, Merle. 'Have You Ever Thought of Making Buttons?' *Lapidary Journal* (San Diego) April 1970

MARTIN, R. *Ballots and Bandwagons*

OSWALD and RUSSEL-SMITH. 'Discovered a Box of Buttons', *The Connoisseur* 1954

PARKE-BERNET. 'Fine Buttons', *Catalogue of an Auction Sale* May 1970

PEACOCK, Primrose. *Hall-Marks on British and Irish Silver* (ESL Bristol) 1970

PERKINS. *Treatise on Haberdashery* 1853 and 1874

RATHBONE, R. L. B. 'Buttons', *The Art Journal* 1909

ROLT, L. T. C. *The Aeronauts* (Longmans 1966)

'The Secret of the Prosperity of Birmingham' (Green, Cadbury and Richards advertising brochure 1876)
SCHULL, T. *Victorian Antiques* (Charles E. Tuttle, Vermont) 1963
SMITH-ALBERT and KENT. *The Complete Button Book* (Doubleday NY) 1949
SMITH-ALBERT and KENT. *The Button Sampler* (Gramercy NY) 1951
Tailor and Cutter May 1952
UNITE JONES, W. *The Button Industry (Common Commodities and Industries)* 1924
WEARIN, O. *Political Campaign Buttons in Color*
WEBB, Lee R. *Early American Pressed Glass* (Lee Publications, Mass) 1960
WEBB, W. M. *The Heritage of Dress* 1907
'What there is in a Button' *Household Words* 1850
Yesterday's Shopping : The Army & Navy Stores Catalogue 1907 (reprinted David & Charles 1970)
ZIM and SCHAFFER. *Rocks and Minerals* (Hamlyn) 1969
36 GEO III c 60

ACKNOWLEDGEMENTS

During the preparation of this book I travelled over 20,000 miles, and met hundreds of people, in Great Britain, the Republic of Ireland, Spain and the United States of America. With one exception they all proved kind, helpful and willing to assist me. Many of them took a great deal of trouble to answer my questions and find the information I required. Without such help this book could never have been completed. It is quite impossible to name each person individually, but special thanks go to Mrs Sally Luscomb and her collector friends at the Just Buttons Museum in America.

In Great Britain and Ireland I approached numerous manufacturers, and all willingly gave assistance, usually at managing director level. I am very flattered and grateful. Special thanks go to Mr Eric Grove of James Grove & Sons Ltd, who allowed me to visit his works and have the photograph taken for plate 12. Others equally kind include Mr T. J. Lawson of the English Glass Company, Mr W. J. Flückiger of Francis Sumner Engineering Ltd, Mr J. L. M. Graham of J & J Cash Ltd, Mr H. Sandon of the Royal Worcester Porcelain Company and Mr J. E. Hartill of Mintons Ltd, to name but a few.

I also visited and corresponded with numerous museums and libraries all over the country. The staff at Birmingham Reference Library and the City Museum and Art Gallery deserve a medal for services to writers, and those at Glastonbury Public Library for being pestered weekly and not complaining!

Finally my sincere thanks to Philip Clarke of *The Sunday Times* who was responsible for introducing me to my publisher, and therefore for the birth of this book.

PHOTOGRAPHS
All photographs except those individually acknowledged were taken by Stephen Essberger of Ross-on-Wye, Herefordshire.